Hindsight

Hindsight

Thirty of the world's
leading designers
give their personal
responses to some of
the most frequently
asked questions
about graphic design

Edited by Ken Cato

CRAFTSMAN HOUSE

Editor Ken Cato
Design Cato Design Inc
Printed by Toppan Singapore

Distributed in Australia by Craftsman House,
Tower A, 112 Talavera Road,
North Ryde, Sydney, NSW 2113
in association with G+B Arts International:
Australia, Canada, China, France, Germany, India,
Japan, Luxembourg, Malaysia, The Netherlands,
Russia, Singapore, Switzerland, United Kingdom,
United States of America

Copyright © 1998 Cato Design Inc.
All rights reserved

ISBN 90 5703 34 10

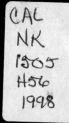

Hindsight may provide new answers to old questions or it may be a starting point for future generations of designers. During the 30 years since my graduation, I have continued to hear the same questions that I heard and asked as a design student. Some of these still cross my mind from time to time. Over the past five years I have gathered a collection of the most-asked questions from over 5000 students of design, and I have sought the assistance of 30 of the world's leading designers to provide some guidance. Like most aspects of design, there is rarely one answer so for each question I have provided a number of different responses; these should be taken as no more than one person's personal opinion. I do not believe that any of the answers is categorically right or wrong. Rather I have tried to provide a guide that can help the reader to decide what is appropriate for them. We all have to make our own decisions and take the road that is right for each of us. Not only have the designers chosen for inclusion in this project made observations that have influenced students of design but their comments have also influenced me and others in our profession. To achieve the broadest possible view, I have tried to balance a number of factors: nationality, background, experiences, design styles and approaches. I strongly believe that the foundation of the profession are the passionate individual beliefs held by its practitioners. It is also this focus and dedication in hindsight that will play a part in guiding the next generation of designers. In years to come, the same questions will be asked but I am sure that new responses will be found. Hopefully we will continue to learn from each other. My thanks to all those who have participated in making this volume possible. KEN CATO

Pierre Bernard

Pierre Bernard was born in Paris in 1942. He studied at the Ecole Supérieure des Arts Décoratifs in Paris and went on to major in poster design at the Warsaw Academy in Poland with the legendary poster designer Henryk Tomaszewski. Before setting up the studio Grapus in 1970, Bernard completed a Masters at the Institute of Environment in Paris. As a collective the group Grapus has received awards and prizes from numerous international competitions including The Warsaw Biennale, Brno Biennale, Lahti Biennale, Zagreb Zgraf, New York Art Directors Club and the Toyama Triennale. Since 1991 Bernard has been working out of the studio Atelier de Création Graphique. Bernard is also teaching at the Ecole Supérieure des Arts Décoratifs in Paris

Alan Chan

Born in 1950, Alan Chan is one of the few Hong Kong-trained graphic designers to achieve international recognition. During his 25 years in advertising and design, he has won more than 300 local and international honours, including awards from Communication Arts, the New York Art Directors Club, Graphis, D& AD, and the Tokyo Type Directors Club. In 1989, Alan was named Designer of the Year by the Hong Kong Artist Guild. In 1980, Alan Chan set up his own company with his wife, Sandra. The company's portfolio comprises a wide variety of work, from corporate identity programmes, packaging and environment design to product design. Chan successfully combines Oriental and Western culture in contemporary graphic design, offering rediscovery and appreciation of traditional Chinese art. He is a regular speaker throughout the East on the subject of cultural identity in graphic design and his work has been widely published in international publications

Garry Emery

Garry Emery is Design Director of Emery Vincent Design, an Australian graphic design firm. A member of Alliance Graphique Internationale, Emery is the recipient of many international honours, including the Gold Award from the Tokyo Typo Directors' Club, and the Gold Award and Silver Awards from the Biennale of Graphic Design, Brno, Czechoslovakia. Emery's distinctive style can be seen in graphics programs for many major public sector projects throughout Australasia such as Australia's new Parliament House in Canberra, Powerhouse Museum in Sydney, Australian Embassies in Tokyo and Beijing, Royal Melbourne Zoological Gardens, Australian National Maritime Museum, Australia Post at Expo '88 and the recently completed Melbourne Exhibition Centre. Emery believes that design cannot be reduced to formula, and neither is there any single design philosophy. He has a real desire to communicate, and he is constantly looking to develop new skills and techniques, including utilising new computer technology

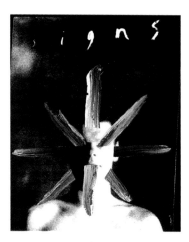

Alan Fletcher

After training at the Royal College of Art in London and the School of Architecture and Design at Yale University, Alan Fletcher's design career began in New York. In 1962 he returned to London setting up Fletcher/Forbes/Gill, before co-founding Pentagram in 1972. Fletcher opened his own studio in 1992, and he is involved with Phaidon Press and Domus Magazine (Milan) as a design consultant. Fletcher has received gold awards from the British Designers & Art Directors Association and the New York 'One Show'. In 1977 he shared the Designers & Art Directors Association President's Award for outstanding contributions to design with Pentagram partner Colin Forbes. He is a Royal Designer for Industry, a Fellow of the Chartered Society of Designers, Senior Fellow of the Royal College of Art. In 1993 Fletcher was awarded The Prince Philip Prize for the Designer of the Year, and in 1994 he was elected to The American Art Directors Club 'Hall of Fame'

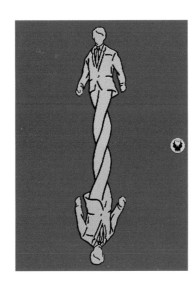

DOWN WITH DOGMA

Shigeo Fukuda

Born in Tokyo in 1932, Shigeo Fukuda graduated from the design course at the Tokyo National University of Fine Arts and Music in 1956. From the start of his career, his work has been awarded worldwide. Ten years after graduating, Fukuda was awarded the Maunishi Industrial Design Award, and at the Brno Biennale he received the Encouragement Award. In 1967 Fukuda held a one-man show at IBM Gallery in New York. Since then Fukuda's distinctive poster designs have continued to capture the judges' attention, winning awards such as the Gold Medal at the International Poster Biennale at Warsaw in 1972, Newcomers Award at the 1976 Art Selection Contest of the Ministry of Education, and a Silver Medal at the Lahti Poster Biennale in 1983. Fukuda is a Director of the Japan Graphic Designers Association, a Committee Member of the Tokyo Art Directors Club, and a member of Alliance Graphique Internationale

Pierre Bernard's cover designs for Signs magazine for the client Total Company
Alan Chan's watches for Alan Chan Creations Ltd
Garry Emery's 3 dimensional objects for Designer's Saturday 1994 for Carmen Furniture
Alan Fletcher's poster for the Chartered Society of Designers entitled 'Down with Dogma'
Shigeo Fukuda's silkscreen poster entitled 'Kintetsu'

Steff Geissbuhler

After working in design in Switzerland, Steff Geissbuhler joined the Faculty of the Philadelphia College of Art, where he was appointed Chairman of the Graphic Design Department. Geissbuhler worked for design firms in Philadelphia and New York before joining Chermayeff & Geissmar in 1975. Geissbuhler's work includes corporate identities and graphics programs for clients such as Time Warner, NBC, Conrad Hotels and the US Environmental Protection Agency. Known for his architectural graphics including work for IBM in New York and the University of Pennsylvania, other assignments include graphics for the Smithsonian Institution's Bicentennial exhibition. Geissbuhler's work has been widely recognised internationally with awards from AIGA, the Art Directors Clubs of New York, Philadelphia and Los Angeles, the International Poster Biennales, and 'The World's Most Memorable Poster' competition in Paris. He has received the US Federal Achievement Design Award and was honoured twice with the First Swiss National Prize for Applied Art

Bob Gill

Bob Gill is one of the world's leading designers. In 1960 he made the decision to go to London, where he remained for 15 years. Together with fellow designers Alan Fletcher and Colin Forbes, Gill started Fletcher/Forbes/Gill, a small design office with a lot of talent and potential that is now known as Pentagram, one of the design industry's leading firms. In 1967 Gill began to work independently in London, returning to New York in 1975 to write and design Beatlemania, which, at that time, was the largest multimedia musical ever on Broadway. 'Forget all the rules you ever learned about graphic design. Including the ones in this book' was published in 1981, and it quickly became required reading in design classes around the world. He was elected to the New York Art Directors Club Hall of Fame in 1991. Gill is still teaching and working independently as a design consultant. His latest book is called 'Graphic Design Made Difficult'

Milton Glaser

Milton Glaser's award-winning career spans four decades and all continents. After establishing Pushpin Studios in 1954, he left to pursue other design work, setting up WBMG, a publication design firm, in 1983. Milton Glaser, Inc. was established in 1974, creating distinctive graphics such as the I Love NY logo; all interior elements, signage and theming of Sesame Place, a children's education park in Pennsylvania; the redesign of a major American supermarket chain for The Grand Union Company, including architectural, interior, packaging and advertising design; the design of an International AIDS Symbol for the World Health Organisation; the design, overall conceptualisation and interior design of New York Unearthed, a museum located in Manhattan's South Street Seaport; and the logo for Tony Kushner's Pulitzer Prize winning play, 'Angels in America'. Glaser is also involved with poster design for numerous international clients. Glaser's work has been exhibited worldwide and is represented in the permanent collections at the Museum of Modern Art, New York; The Israel Museum, Jerusalem; The Chase Manhattan Bank, New York; and the National Archive, Smithsonian Institute, Washington, DC

Roz Goldfarb

Roz Goldfarb established Roz Goldfarb Associates, Inc. (RGA International) in 1985, specialising in the recruitment of creative and managerial personnel for graphic design, advertising, new media and multimedia. As well as her extensive business management experience, Goldfarb served as Director of Pratt Institute's Associate Degree Programs (The Pratt Phoenix School of Design). Goldfarb is the author of 'Careers by Design', and she is a frequent speaker for professional groups, including The International Design Conference at Aspen. She has also lectured at The School of Visual Arts, Art Center College of Design (as a Toyota Scholar), The Parsons School of Design and Pratt Institute. In 1987 Goldfarb set up a scholarship with the Art Directors Club of New York to further the education of talented design students. Goldfarb holds a Master of Fine Arts from Pratt Institute and a Bachelor of Arts from Hunter College of the City University of New York. She is a member of The Board of Advisors of FIT/State University of New York in New York City

Takenobu Igarashi

Takenobu Igarashi is a designer and sculptor of international renown. A graduate of Tama Art University in Tokyo, Igarashi obtained a Master of Arts in Art from the University of California, Los Angeles. Igarashi Studio was established in 1970 creating work that includes graphic design, industrial design and sculpture. His signature style can be seen in his series of axonometric posters using alphabets and letterforms, as well as shopping bags and calendars for The Museum of Modern Art, New York, (MoMA). Igarashi's work also includes corporate identities for Meiji Milk Products and Suntory Limited, 'The Hibiki' sculpture at the entrance of Suntory Hall in Tokyo, limited edition sculptures for the Nissan 'Infiniti' showrooms in the US, the 'Legame' cordless telephone for Folmer Co. Ltd., and YMD products for Yamada Shomei Lighting Co. Ltd. He lectures regularly at various institutions and conferences, and his work is included in the permanent collection of MoMA, New York, as well as other museums and universities throughout the world. Recent publications include 'Rock, Scissors, Paper' and 'Igarashi Sculptures'

Steff Geissbuhler's brochures for the New York Public Library
Bob Gill's poster for the New York Art Directors Club
Milton Glaser's poster for Campari Bitter for Davide-Campari, Milano
Takenobu Igarashi's magazine cover for the Japan Industrial Design Promotion Organisation

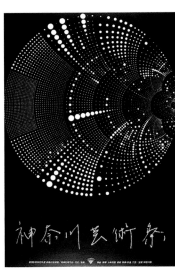

Tibor Kalman

After moving to the US in 1956 to study journalism at New York University, Kalman never completed the course. His career in design began when he went on to work as a Design Director at Barnes and Noble Bookstores. Kalman started M&Co in 1979, working in the areas of industrial design and architecture magazines, and becoming involved with film directing and design for television. From 1994 to late 1995 Kalman worked as Editor in Chief for the Benetton sponsored 'Colours' magazine. His work is represented in the permanent collections of the Museum of Modern Art, New York, The Stedelijk Museum, Amsterdam, The Museum fur Gestaltung, Zurich, and the Victoria & Albert Museum, London

Tibor Kalman's cover for
'Colors' magazine
David Lancashire's magazine design
for Dalton Fine Paper
Mary Lewis's packaging design
for Oban Distillery
Shin Matsunaga's poster for
the Japan Graphic Designers
Association Inc
Jennifer Morla's poster for the
California College of Arts & Crafts

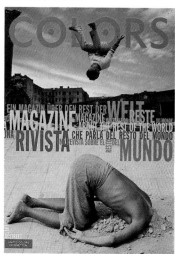

David Lancashire

After studying fine art in the UK, David Lancashire settled in Australia working for large advertising agencies and design studios before starting his own firm. Over the years Lancashire has undertaken various design projects including work for clients such as Mercedes Benz, Dulux, Kodak, Berri Estates, BHP, Safeway, Australian Airlines, Australian Nature Conservation Agency (Federal Government), Amcal Chemists, McCain Foods, Myer, Sportsgirl Australia, Oberoi Hotels International and J. Wattie Foods. Lancashire's work has appeared in many graphic design publications both in Australia and Europe, and he has won awards including one from the Goethe Institute (Library Promotions Council). The Library commissioned his work four years running from 1984. Lancashire has been President of the Australian Graphic Design Association (Victoria), a member of the Advisory Committee of the Department of Photography at the Royal Melbourne Institute of Technology, and he is currently on the Stamp Advisory Board of Australia Post and the Graphic Design Advisory Committee for Phillip Institute of Technology

Mary Lewis (UK)

Mary Lewis is recognised as one of Britain's leading packaging designers. Her fresh, sophisticated style has universal appeal. In 1984 Lewis founded Lewis Moberly with Robert Moberly and the result is an abundance of awards, including the DBA Design Effectiveness Award and a British D&AD Gold Award for Outstanding Design. Lewis' work includes projects for United Distillers Classic Malts and Royal Mail Special Stamps. She is now a member of the Royal Mail Stamps Committee, President of the British D&AD and a Fellow of The Royal Chartered Society of Designers

Shin Matsunaga

Shin Matsunaga graduated from Tokyo National University of Fine Arts and Music in 1964, majoring in Visual Design He established Shin Matsunaga Design Inc. in 1971. His work has been internationally acclaimed, winning a special award from the Japan Advertising Artists Club early in his career. Matsunaga has received many other awards including Tokyo Art Directors Club Awards, a Gold Medal at the Japanese Graphic Design Exhibition in New York and many international medals and prizes for poster design. Matsunaga is also widely known for his 1986 peace poster, his art direction and graphic design work for the Sezon Museum of Art, design for the bestselling book 'The Visual Constitution of Japan', packaging for well-known products such as 'Scotties' tissues and 'Blendy' coffee, and corporate identities for Issey Miyake and Rihga Royal Hotels. Matsunaga's work is included in the permanent collection of the Museum of Modern Art in New York and other museums around the world. In 1995 he held one-man show of new drawings, and sculptures, 'Freaks', in Tokyo

Jennifer Morla

Jennifer Morla is President and Creative Director of Morla Design. She has been honoured internationally for her ability to pair wit and elegance on everything from annual reports to music videos. She has received over 500 awards for excellence in graphic design and was declared one of the fifteen masters of design by 'How' magazine. Morla's work is a part of the permanent collection of the San Francisco Museum of Modern Art and the Library of Congress, and has also been displayed at the Grand Palais in Paris and the Brandenburg Art Gallery in Berlin. Most recently, her work was featured in a solo exhibition in Osaka, Japan. In addition to teaching senior graphic design at California College of Arts and Crafts, she paints, sculpts, and creates site-specific installations

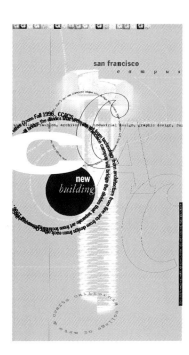

John Nowland

John Nowland Design was established in 1974 in Adelaide, Australia. Under the guidance of founder John Nowland, the company covers all aspects of graphic design from design development to application, including tendering, scheduling and supervision, or printing or manufacture. Working from purpose-built premises, Nowland's company work both individually and in teams with other consultants to find appropriate solutions to communication problems. The company's work is diverse, utilising its depth and range of design expertise in the areas of corporate identities, stationery, corporate communications, profiles, annual reports, literature, packaging, signage, exhibitions, books, and promotional and informative literature

Vaughan Oliver

Vaughan Oliver studied graphic design at Newcastle upon Tyne Polytechnic. After moving to London in 1980, Oliver worked at Benchmark before joining Michael Peters and Partners where he met Ivo Watts-Russell, the founder of the independent record company 4AD. For three years he did freelance work for the label and by 1983, Oliver had become 4AD's full-time in-house designer. Oliver is also the founder of 23 Envelope, which produces some of the most notable design for the music industry. In 1988 Oliver went freelance, adopting the new studio name V23, whilst he continued to work for 4AD. Oliver's work for V23 includes music industry commissions, a publishing project, a television channel identity and programme titles, publicity posters, magazine design and various book jackets. V23 recently completed its first television commercial work for clients Microsoft, Converse and Sony. Since the establishment of V23, Oliver's work has been widely exhibited internationally, and he held his first English exhibition in Newcastle upon Tyne in 1996

Michael Peters

Michael Peters graduated from Yale with a Masters Degree in Fine Art in 1964. He worked for CBS Television in New York before setting up Michael Peters and Partners in 1970; by 1983 the company had become one of the largest design firms in the world and was quoted on the London Stock Exchange. Peters has won numerous awards for his work all over the world, and is a frequent lecturer and writer on the role of design in the prediction of future trends. In 1992 Peters formed Identica, a totally new design and communications consultancy linked to a science and technology centre in Cambridge. Identica specialises in corporate literature, corporate identities, consumer innovation and communication, and corporate software. The combination of Michael Peters' vision, and the cumulative talents of the strategic, design and implementation teams, ensures that clients are given design solutions of the highest quality, relevance and value for money

Jean Robert

Jean Robert was born in Switzerland and he studied at L'Ecole Des Arts et Mèteriers in La Chaux-de-Fonds. Immediately after graduation, Robert commenced work as a graphic designer for Pirelli Industries in Milan. By 1971 Robert was working for Unimark International in London, moving to Pentagram as Senior Designer by 1972. After five years, he returned to Switzerland, opening his own graphic design studio with his partner Kati Durrer In Zurich working on many different projects from packaging and corporate identities to designing the Swatch range of watches. Robert is a member of Alliance Graphique Internationale and the Switzerland Art Director's Club, and his work has been included in several international exhibitions. He has also been a guest lecturer at the Ohio State University, and was a teacher at the School of Design in Zurich. Robert's work has been published in IDEA Magazine and Graphis

Brian Sadgrove

Brian Sadgrove is Principal of Brian Sadgrove and Associates, a Melbourne-based design firm. After studying at the Royal Melbourne Institute of Technology, Sadgrove worked as an Editorial Designer at BHP and the Department of Trade, and later as an art director at USP and J Walter Thompson. In 1968 Sadgrove commenced private practice as a graphic designer working on currency and stamp design amongst other projects. The firm has won numerous awards in Australia and overseas, and its work has been represented in most major design publications including 'Graphis', 'IDEA Magazine', 'Design', 'Design World' (Australia) 'Design Down Under', and it has been featured in the Powerhouse Museum in Sydney. Sadgrove served as a member of the Stamp Advisory Board, and he is a member of the Course Advisory Board of Swinburne University, the Australian Design Academy, AGDA, the Design Institute of Australia, and he is a fellow of the Industrial Design Institute of Australia

John Nowland's pre-stamped envelope design for Australia Post
Vaughan Oliver's poster for 4Ad entitled 'All Virgos are Mad'
Michael Peter's logotype for Building & Property Service Management
Jean Robert's designs for Swatch
Brian Sadgrove's packaging design for Solana wine for Bodegas & Bebidas, Spain

Makoto Saito

Makoto Saito's multi award-winning work has earned him an international reputation. He has received numerous Tokyo Art Directors Club Awards, including the Tokyo ADC Grand Prix in 1995. Saito's poster designs have also received awards such as the Grand Prix at the France International Poster Exhibition in 1990, a silver medal at the Brno Biennale in 1990, Second Prize at International Poster Exhibition, Chaumont in 1993, Bronze at the 4th International Poster Triennale in Toyama in 1994, and the Good Design Awards in 1995 (Chicago Athenaeum). His work is included in the collections of the Museum of Modern Art, New York, the National Museum of Modern Art, Munich, the Warsaw Poster Museum, the Lahti Poster Museum, the Brandenburg Art Museum, the Tokyo Museum of Art and the Chicago Museum. Makoto Saito is a member of the Tokyo Art Director's Club, Tokyo Designer's Space, Japan Art Graphic Designer's Association and Alliance Graphique Internationale

Erik Spiekermann

Erik Spiekermann studied Art History at university, running a printing press for a living. He moved to London in 1973 where he started designing typefaces and writing books about typography. After seven years in London, Spiekermann returned to Berlin to set up MetaDesign, now Germany's largest design firm, employing more than 80 designers. Since 1992 MetaDesign has also had an office in San Francisco and, since August 1995, another office in London. He travels the world as the typographic evangelist and considers designing complex information systems as his hobby

Henry Steiner

Henry Steiner was born in 1934 in Vienna, raised in New York, educated at Hunter College, Yale University, and the Sorbonne. He founded Graphic Communication Ltd (later Steiner & Co) in Hong Kong 1964. Under his direction the company has become one of the leading worldwide design consultancies, producing annual reports, corporate identity programs and packaging. His work has won many international awards and has been represented in numerous books and periodicals. Steiner has been a President of Alliance Graphique Internationale, Fellow of the Chartered Society of Designers and the New York Art Directors Club, and a member of the American Institute of Graphic Arts. His work has exerted a marked influence on design in Asia, and he has co-authored a new book, 'Cross-Cultural Design' published by Thames & Hudson

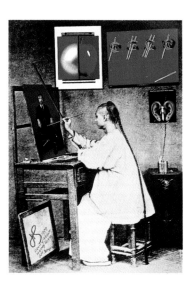

Deborah Sussman

Deborah Sussman's career began with Charles and Ray Eames, eventually opening her own office in Los Angeles in 1968. Sussman/Prejza & Co. Inc. was formed in 1980 with clients such as Hasbro Inc., Disney Development and Apple Computers. The firm led the development of the environmental graphics for the 1984 Olympic Games in Los Angeles, considered a milestone in the history of urban graphics. Sussman is an Honorary member and Fellow of several professional societies, including AIA, SEGD, and ACD. In 1995 she was honoured as the 7th designer to exhibit in New York's School of Visual Arts 'Master Series'. Sussman's current work includes urban identity and streetscape programs, graphics and interiors for the New Jersey Performing Arts Center, several sports arenas, and the identity program for the new publishing company, Knowledge Exchange. S/P has been featured in 'Interiors' magazine, and is the subject of a 144-page monograph recently published by Process Architecture

Barrie Tucker

Barrie Tucker is one of Australia's leading designers. His work includes poster design, corporate identities and packaging. Tucker's work has been included in several exhibitions worldwide such as 'L'Etiquette de vin', Switzerland, 'World Peace Flag' Exhibition at World Expo 1992 in Spain, and 'Gitanes, Silhouette' at the Georges Pompidou Centre, Paris, and some is on permanent display at the ICOGRADA Permanent Collection, London, the Museum for Art and Crafts, Hamburg, Germany, the German Poster Museum, Essen, and the 'People to People' collage/mural, UNESCO World Headquarters in Paris. His work also formed a solo exhibition 'The Design World of Barrie Tucker' Retrospective Exhibition at the AXIS Gallery, Tokyo. Tucker is a Fellow of the Design Institute of Australia his work has been published in international design magazines and annuals. Tucker has won numerous awards, including several CLIO's and awards for poster and packaging design

Makoto Saito's poster for the fashion house Alpha Cubic
Henry Steiner's poster entitled 'Self-Image' for Artspec Imaging Ltd, New Zealand
Erik Spiekermann's stamp design for PTT Netherlands
Deborah Sussman's logotype used on a poster for the School of Visual Arts, New York
Barrie Tucker's packaging design for Octavius I for S. Smith & Son

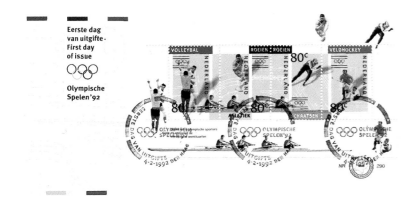

Michael Vanderbyl

Michael Vanderbyl is Dean of the School of Design at California College of Arts and Crafts. He is Principal of Vanderbyl Design, a multi-disciplinary firm. Vanderbyl has gained international prominence in the design field as a practitioner, educator, critic and advocate, and he was featured on the PBS series 'The Creative Mind'. Vanderbyl has served on the National Board of Directors of the AIGA, The AIGA Education Committee, and is a founding member of the AIGA, San Francisco Chapter. Vanderbyl holds a position on the Design Advisory Board and the Accession Committee at the San Francisco Museum of Modern Art. and he is a member of Alliance Graphique Internationale. Vanderbyl's work can be seen in the permanent collections of museums around the world. Vanderbyl's Design is featured in numerous publications including 'Seven Graphic Designers', 'First Choice' and both Graphis and Graphis Poster Annuals (Switzerland). Vanderbyl 's work has also been published internationally in 'Abitare', 'IDEA' Magazine and 'Novum Gerbrauchsgraphik'. In the US, his work has appeared in 'CA', AIGA Annuals, 'Interiors', 'Design Issues', 'Metropolis' and 'Time' Graphis

Massimo Vignelli

Massimo Vignelli studied architecture in Milan and Venice. In 1965 Vignelli co-founded Unimark International Corporation, and, with Lella Vignelli, he established Vignelli Associates in 1971, and Vignelli Designs in 1978. His work has been published and exhibited extensively, notably at the Museum of Modern Art, the Metropolitan Museum of Art, the Cooper-Hewitt Museum, the Musèe Des Arts Décoratifs in Montreal, and Die Neue Sammlung in Munich. Vignelli has taught and lectured in major cities and universities throughout the world. He is a past president of Alliance Graphique Internationale and the AIGA, a Vice President of The Architectural League, and a member of IDSA. Among Vignelli's many awards are the first Presidential Design Award, presented by President Ronald Reagan in 1985, the National Arts Club Gold Medal for Design, and the Interior Product Designers Fellowship of Excellence, 1992. He has been awarded an Honorary Doctorate in Architecture from the University of Venice, and Honorary Doctorates in Fine Arts from Parsons School of Design, Pratt Institute, Rhode Island School of Design, and Corcoran School of Art

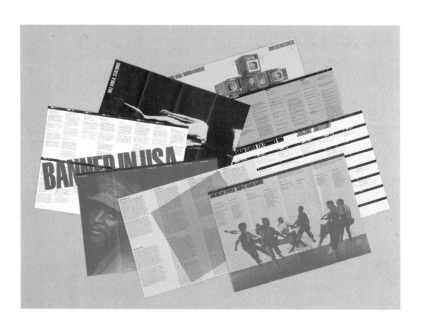

John Warwicker

John Warwicker is one of the co-founders of the dynamic London-based creative studio, Tomato. Established in 1991, Tomato employs an holistic approach to design within a contemporary cultural context. Drawing on myriad influences, from language and philosophy to traditional art, the success of Tomato lies in its diversity of talent and experience. Work ranges from typographic design to music video productions as well as graphic design. Members of Tomato have always subscribed to an open objective, following individual projects to find new forms of expression and structure. Working as a collective organisation, Tomato has become involved with all forms of media and design to produce the spontaneous design that gets an immediate response. John Warwicker completed an Honours degree in Graphic Design in London before continuing his work and research into electronic media and its effects on communication, culture and the community

Mark Wickens

Mark Wickens is Chairman and Creative Director of Wickens Tutt Southgate. After graduating from Kingston in 1982 he worked for Michael Peters & Partners for eight years as a Design Group Head. In this time Wickens gained valuable experience in packaging design for clients such as Bass, Rank Hovis McDougall, Seagram and Unilever. In 1989, after leaving Michael Peters & Associates, he formed Wickens Tutt Southgate. Now Britain's fourth largest design company, Wickens' company has established a reputation for ambitious and individual design, and are positioned as one of the UK's leaders in packaging design. Clients include Britvic, Gossard, Seagram and SmithKline Beecham. Wickens is a Member of D&AD and his work has been recognised around the world

Michael Wolff

Michael Wolff is co-founder and former creative director of Wolff Olins, having recently held the positions of Chairman and Creative Director of Addison. Wolff has also been President of both the D&AD and the CSD. Among his clients are Apple (The Beatles, not the computers), BOC, Bovis, BP, Newell & Sorrell, Renault, 3i, Saab, Shell Oil, Volkswagon Audi and P&O

Michael Vanderbyl's poster for the San Francisco Museum of Modern Art
Massimo Vignelli's corporate literature for the American Centre in Paris
John Warwicker's stills from a video designed with Tomato
Michael Wolff's symbol for Addison Design Consultants
Mark Wicken's packaging design for Tango for Britvic

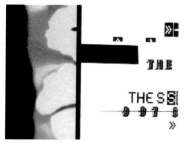

'My philosophy was simply to earn a living by designing. I guess it's when you don't have to do it for a living, but continue to that the philosophy has to be a little deeper. Because to me there seems to be so much of everything, it's nice to be a reductionist, to do as much as possible with as little as possible. To edit and focus design resolutions so that in their own way they are eloquent and not a victim of fashion'

Brian Sadgrove

While regional differences in graphic design certainly exist it is interesting to note that the kind of questions that plague students are universal. In fact I'm not sure one should separate the student questions from the 'professional's' and students should take comfort in the knowledge that they are not alone in what may seem as personal and professional confusion. Certainly within my experiences lecturing to students and professional alike, I find the question and answer sessions amazingly similar. Everyone is confronted with the same dilemmas and apprehensions. Questions always seem to focus on how to move a career forward; how to find, maintain and keep a client; how to present work; how to price it; how to convince the clients as to the intrinsic benefits of 'good design'; and in the last analysis how do you begin to define 'good design'. Part of my role as a recruiter of talent for graphic design is to advise people on the current qualifications required for employment. In my day-to-day responsibilities as consultant to my clients I often find myself acting as a barometer of not only what's happening 'out there' but often finding that I can identify emerging trends for future business directions. My office is positioned in an unusual corner of the market-place and it's strength is that our clients are extremely diversified in both their work speciality as well as their geographical location. They are the business leaders of marketing communications firms, corporations and advertising agencies. And the questions often asked by our clients interested in our ability to take the 'temperature' of our industry are mirrored in the questions we are asked by students and professional at seminars. So while our scope can be broad, for the purposes of this short essay, I will confine myself to

questions relating to portfolios, resumes and what our clients ask for when they need to hire. They are probably the most critical areas of importance to designers in the early years of their careers and seeking employment.

Portfolio content is always the primary concern of everyone. Here's my rule of thumb in a nutshell: a portfolio is always as strong as the weakest link. Consistency of work has to be an abiding goal. A portfolio of uneven quality will be criticised and usually turned down. Regardless how long or short the presentation, a portfolio's many excellent pieces will suffer by comparison to the weaker work. Any inconsistencies can be deadly. The standard set by the better works might establish the overall level of performance. Perhaps it is the highly critical nature of creative people or perhaps it is because we are all trained to immediately focus on what can be redefined or corrected. In any case, a portfolio has to be carefully analysed and critique (preferably by an objective third party) to determine any inconsistencies in quality. It is very difficult for a creative person to objectively view their own work. Usually only time can provide the proper critical distance. I have often been asked 'Why was that item included?' and the inclusion of a weak link it is often interpreted as a lack of taste on the part of the designer. Your taste level (always a highly subjective topic) is what is being tested. Never mind that perhaps the designer wanted to show a variety of experience. Therefore if you have ever worked on a project that you didn't admire but want to include in your presentation to demonstrate practical work experience, be sure to label it accordingly and place it in a separate part of your portfolio, separating it from your creative work. The size of a portfolio and your method of presentation is totally up to you. It can be anything, as long as it 'works'. This means it has to be logical and the structure has to relate to the function of the work exhibited. That's what makes it 'work'. I'll discuss more about presentation soon, but remember, there are no absolute answers and do not trust anyone who tells you it has to be one way or another. However, portfolios are traditionally not long on content and simple in presentation style. I have always thought of a portfolio as a kind of visual psychological short hand to the viewer that states where you have been (your experience) and where you would like to go (your future). It's structure send all kinds of subtle messages about how you perceive yourself and your work. Most likely a portfolio (or book in our vernacular) should contain no more that 20 samples and no less than 10. However it is totally individualistic dependent on interests, experience and competence. As long as all the work is worth showing! It's good to start with your strongest piece for it creates an atmosphere of excitement and anticipation for the viewer to want to see more. Your presentation should be organised and immaculate. How you treat your work tells the viewer not only the respect you show to your creativity but how you will probably treat that company's work. While you want to show professional quality, finished pieces, you should always include drawings and/or sketches that show process. No one I know, and who I respect, wants to see a book that only shows finished and printed work. They need to see how you think, not what was accepted by a client. Remember, do not become so dependent on technology that you cannot provide those important thumbnails and don't make the mistake of throwing them away, thinking they are no longer important.

The portfolio presentation should be, as stated, logical to it's subject matter (ie two dimensional or three dimensional projects have different requirements) and size of projects and should always be impeccably neat and clean. The actual structure (ring-binder, boards, transparencies) are all options. Combining formats is always an option as long as it's logical. Small and large transparencies are generally of a good quality, they are not heavy as a portfolio of many board mounted samples (ask anyone who has carried them can tell you), they work well with three dimensional or large scale projects, and they can be packed into a fairly small case. A small case has advantages of being light and easily transportable, especially if you need to ship it or carry it on a plane. And of course they cost less, always an advantage! I also ask for actual printed work (if you have it) as nothing surpasses the touch, smell and feel of a well-printed piece. Again, don't forget to include a folder or special pocket labelled sketches with those important roughs showing process and thinking. Whatever formats you may choose, remember to keep the structure flexible. Flexibility will allow you to change the order or pieces or to remove or exchange prices. It is always best to research the firm that you approval for work. Know ahead of time what kind of work they do and then be sure to show applicable work in your portfolio towards the front of your book. It also sends a message that you understand their business and that you want to participate in it. Lastly make sure everything is properly labelled. Your name and a place you can be contacted should be on the outside of your portfolio as a luggage tag as well as on the inside (tags can fall off). Your name should be on every sample as well, in case a piece is for any reason removed.

Your portfolio should always include a resume. While this is not to be an in-depth analysis of resume structures, there are some distinct priorities for graphic designers I would like you to consider. First of all, as with your graphic samples, your resume should be exceptionally well laid out as a piece of informational communication. It should communicate something about your personal style, simple and direct. It should furthermore be totally devoid of any typo's or mis-spellings. Make sure you have another person look at it. Spell-checking on a computer is not enough! A resume should be divided into several sections showing 1) education (only college and advanced degrees or specialised programs), 2) work experience, 3) related experience (work study programs, internships, summer jobs), 4) special skills and/or language expertise, 5) special awards. When referring to any work experience a resume should mention the kind and quality of project responsibility as well as the name of the clients. For example, if you were to simply say that you worked for the ABC company as a graphic designer, one would not know if you produced corporate identities or packages or corporate literature. In addition the reader would not know if you completed projects assigned to you by another person or if you had responsibility for ideation and implementation. You should include a brief description of your full responsibilities; ie. did you work with vendors, photographers, illustrators, budgets, supervise others, etc. When you indicate your education be sure to include your date of graduation and degree awarded. If you did not complete your course of study, show the years you did attend. Please avoid including any pictures of yourself as well as interests and hobbies. We all love travel and good food and it doesn't belong on your resume. If your personal interests include something that impacts on you professionally, it's another matter. Resumes can sometimes be pretty strange. We once got a resume that indicated the person could finish a Cube in 60 seconds and another that listed a sex change as 'born and born again'. Finally, after you have mastered your perfect resume and portfolio presentation, you are ready for the all-important interview. What is it that people want? It's good to put yourself in the other person's position, understand their frustration's and think about the process objectively. Let's first talk about what they don't

want. I think that most employers are so busy and over-loaded with their own responsibilities, the last thing they want is another person who will be demanding upon their time and energy. They want help that's reliable and trustworthy. Therefore they are constantly telling us that they can't have anybody on board who has an 'attitude'. They demand (and should receive) someone who wants to work hard, who is dedicated, who is a team-player, who is talented but can also take direction, and lastly someone who is ambitious and wants to grow with the company. The secret ingredient of all however is passion. A passion for the work and a passion for the business is found in too few people. It really makes a difference. but of course this is a complete description of you! None-the-less, you have to be able to communicate it in the interview. Your enthusiasm and energy must be apparent as well as your ability to communicate verbally. Your verbal and written skills are every bit as important as your creative abilities. Design is first and foremost a business and you have to hone your skills to deal with other people, both those to whom you report, as well as those who will report to you. Today firms are increasingly sophisticated as to the marketing strategies that drive design solutions. The companies that are the clients are increasingly broadening their markets and geographical scope. Technology has removed a lot of the excesses of redundant staff. The individual who will succeed in this environment has to have a business savvy as well as a creative talent. This individual has to be able to create a visual solution to a marketing need or strategy and to be able to present the reasons why the solutions work to the client in a convincing manner. Furthermore this individual has to be mindful to budget and deadlines, be able to supervise others and to perhaps speak other languages. Certainly this person needs to be knowledgeable of cross cultural needs in an international business environment. I hope this person is you and I wish you success.

Roz Goldfarb

Q

What is about the right amount of pieces that I should have in my portfolio? What do you think is more important, showing thought processes or highly finished pieces?

'Between ten and fifteen pieces showing thought processes. I recommend a few, a minimum of five, that are finished in an appropriate manner for a presentation. For example, packaging, corporate identity, stationery, annual report, exhibition/display and the remainder showing the development and resolution of an idea'

John Nowland

'We want to see where the idea came from, how it evolved, what got discarded along the way and why? Why the end result looks the way it does and how you and the client feel about it'

Erik Spiekermann

'I assume this question relates to the portfolios of those fresh out of school without much professional experience. The right number of pieces is determined by how many projects demonstrate your ability to solve problems. And how many are solutions you feel good and strong about. Anything you have to make excuses for or need to explain too much should be eliminated. Showing your thought processes is always more important than showing highly finished pieces. However it is important to show positive and comprehensive solutions, executed with craftsmanship, accuracy and perfection'

Steff Geissbuhler

Steff Geissbuhler's poster for the Department of Cultural Affairs, New York
Right Garry Emery's catalogue for 'Workshop 3000/Susan Cohn', a Japanese exhibition

'The fewer pieces the better. It is most important to demonstrate process and attitude. The processes of design, of thinking, developing ideas and refining and realising them, are critical indications of a designer's calibre. Attitude is also a major factor in success; good designers have to be unusually tenacious, driven, obsessive, fastidious, flexible, pragmatic, enthusiastic, curious and resourceful. What you cannot afford is complacency'

Garry Emery

'No·one in their right mind hires your portfolio. They hire you. In any case what you did before doesn't really show what you could do in the future.

The only point of a portfolio is to illustrate the points you want to make about yourself and your strengths and weaknesses. For instance, if you're great at teamwork and poor at detail show a project that demonstrates good teamwork and describe how it all happened.

If you're good at creating lots of concepts quickly, show lots of concepts; if you're good at detail, show amazing detail. Use the pieces in your portfolio to illustrate the key qualities that you feel you can bring to a job. That way you can show people how you communicate the idea of you and make it easier to choose you at the same time'

Michael Wolff

Bob Gill, formerly blah, blah, blah, blah, blah, blah, blah, blah, blah, blah, blah, blah, blah, blah, blah, blah and blah.
Founded blah, blah, blah, blah, blah, blah, blah, blah, blah, blah, blah, blah, blah, blah, blah, blah, blah, blah and blah.
Awarded a blah, blah, blah, blah, blah, blah, blah, blah, blah, blah, blah and blah.
He recently blah, blah, blah, blah, blah, blah, blah, blah, blah, blah, blah, blah and blah, blah, blah, blah, blah, blah, blah.
He then blah, blah, blah, blah, blah, blah, blah and is now available for design and advertising projects at One Fifth Ave., New York, NY 10003. Tel: 212 460 0950.

'Your portfolio should consist of the work that **you think** is the best work. Don't worry about what others think. Even if you want to show people what they want to see, you'll probably get it wrong'

Bob Gill

'Only one piece would be ideal!
However, this type of arrogance is very
risky, even if the concept is excellent
and the execution flawless; this is trying
to impress one's interviewer too
much. Otherwise, less than twenty
pieces is appropriate'

Pierre Bernard

'Your portfolio should contain 14-20
pieces. In using the word 'piece' I mean
projects of varying lengths and levels
of complexity. Each piece should show
variety in ways of working, such as 2D
and 3D. Show your conceptual skills
as well as your ability to do mock-up
because in the beginning your first job
will involve the implementation of
other peoples' concepts'

Michael Vanderbyl

Opposite Pierre Bernard's cover
design for 'Tatagumi Yokogumi'
('Horizontal and Vertical')
a Japanese magazine
Left John Warwicker's stills from
a video designed with Tomato
Michael Vanderbyl's promotional
brochure for Champion Papers'
Subjective Reasoning Series

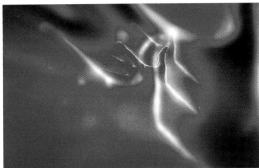

'Intention and karma are the most
important things'

John Warwicker

'There is no ideal number. It depends
on what you want to show. And show
finished pieces'

Massimo Vignelli

Q

How did you get
into the profession?
In your own
experience did you
have to 'talk
nonsense' to get
to certain positions
or jobs?

Opposite Milton Glaser's poster
for LaGuardia Community College
Jean Robert's signage for Devon, a
jewellery shop and gallery, designed
with his partner Kati Durrer

'I can't imagine thinking of this activity as an industry. I always think of it as being halfway between a religious calling and a craft. I am quite certain I talked nonsense (and still do) to get certain positions for a job but sadly I am not aware of when I'm talking nonsense. At that moment I always think I'm telling the truth'
Milton Glaser

'By offering my services to a wide range of clients, by looking into their business and their needs and offering the best solution. And no, you don't have to talk nonsense instead you must communicate'
Massimo Vignelli

'So far the clients we work for do not appreciate us 'talking nonsense' to provide their design solution. If they think we talk nonsense they are certainly at the wrong address'
Jean Robert

20TH ANNIVERSARY 1974/1994
A PROMISE KEPT

MIDDLE COLLEGE HIGH SCHOOL
At LaGuardia Community College/CUNY

Presents
the
July
19
pale saints
20
unrest
his name is alive
21
underground lovers
22
red house painters
23
the wolfgang press
24
brendan perry
heidi berry

'I got into the industry by deciding to tell people I was a designer and asking for meetings to discuss possible work. I decided that I had the talent and had always been a designer from the age of two. I reached the point where I needed to earn money and I went for jobs where people employed designers. I never claimed to have experience when I didn't. I was always, and hopefully will always be, willing to learn. As for nonsense, you never know if you're talking nonsense or not. One man's nonsense is another man's enlightenment and vice-versa. I do know that there's never any point in dishonesty. It can become an addictive way of operating and it's enormously destructive because it precludes trust. It never works'
Michael Wolff

'My ambition as a graphics graduate was to specialise in illustration but when commissions weren't forthcoming I was sidetracked into a 'day job' as junior designer in a packaging design studio. There I got hooked on typography and because I'd never learnt the rules at college, it was easy to break them. Whisky labels and baked bean cans weren't the ideal forum for that but freelance commissions from Ivo Watts-Russel who was setting up his own independent record label provided the opportunity. We'd coincide at the same gigs and I liked his sincere and qualitative approach as well as the music he was releasing, so I joined him in 1983 at 4AD, his first employee. I never felt obliged to 'talk nonsense' in pursuit of my professional ambitions though I am quite capable of doing so, and I apparently oblige on occasion, if querulous and bemused expressions are anything to go by'
Vaughan Oliver

'I entered design through the back doors of advertising in Adelaide, Melbourne and, more importantly in Zurich. This is where an advertising agency was also heavily involved in designing brochures, reports, posters, invitations, conferences and books, as well as ads. To 'talk nonsense' will never get a designer anywhere, except out the door backwards! Certainly I have had more than a good share of nonsense talked to me, or at me, but the only way to win a handsome design project, and to build up a good rapport and an ongoing relationship, is first, to listen and second, to talk absolute sense.

All business people are there to make themselves and their business a success. They only wish to know how you as a designer can help make that happen! If you talk nonsense you will give nothing to the job and/or project being discussed. Successfully do the job in a sensible, positive manner! All successful designers have earned their status because of their high quality achievements'
Barrie Tucker

Opposite Vaughan Oliver's poster promoting a 4AD music festival (Detail) Barrie Tucker's packaging for Woods Bagot's 125 Year Anniversary Muscat, designed with Hans Kohla

Alan Chan's packaging range
for Optical Shop

'Since I was a teenager, I have always had an interest in drawing and I appreciated all pretty and nicely designed items. After graduating from secondary school as a science student, I sent off my application letters to all the local advertising agencies hoping at least one would offer me a job. Simultaneously, I attended a ten-month evening course on graphic design to learn the skills required for this type of job. In my own experience, talking nonsense gets you nowhere especially when you are green. It is better to be honest as people do not expect you to be experienced anyway'
Alan Chan

'Through my friends.
No, you don't have to talk nonsense'
Takenobu Igarashi

Takenobu Igarashi's packaging for the
Museum of Modern Art, New York
Opposite Brian Sadgrove's logotype
for Cinema Nova, Melbourne

'In the middle part of this century, in Melbourne, formal qualifications did not seem necessary. At nights I studied an eclectic mix of accounting, sculpture, drawing and industrial design at Caulfield Tech. (now Monash University) and Royal Melbourne Institute of Technology (RMIT). My first 'design' job was designing a bi-monthly publication called BHP Review. I think I was employed because I didn't look like an artist. This also applied for my second job with the Commonwealth Department of Trade as Publications Designer. I think there was a bit of fast talk for my two jobs as an Art Director at USP and J. Walter Thompson. These days, as Principal of a design practice I try not to talk nonsense but it's hard to tell'
Brian Sadgrove

CINEMA

NOVA

Dettling
Kirschwasser
Eau de Vie de
Cerises Noires
Maturité et
Pureté
Garanties
Maison
Fondée
1 8 6 7
Dettling
KIRSCH
1980
EN 1867
Dettling
Kirschwasser
Eau de Vie de
Cerises Noires
Pureté
Garanties
Maison

'I don't start with 'what do I want'. One of the valuable aspects of what I do is the variety. Briefs come in all shapes and sizes. Clients are sophisticated and naive, institutionalised and individualistic. I like it this way. It avoids a formal or indulgent approach. I love design but I hate compromise. And I could be described as 'tough' about that'

Mary Lewis

'Very. There's no question that you have to fight long and hard to keep up your standards and get your concepts accepted. The people I envy are those who are bastards inside but somehow come across like easy-going sweethearts. They have the interpersonal skills I struggle to attain'

Henry Steiner

'Very tough, but for a good reason. Quality control is your responsibility'

Massimo Vignelli

Q

How tough and demanding do you have to be to get what you want and the jobs you want in the industry?

Henry Steiner's book jacket design for 'Cross Cultural Design' (Thames & Hudson)
Below Mary Lewis's logotype for Heals, a US department store
Opposite Mary Lewis's packaging for Dettling Kirschwasser

HEAL'S

San Fran
cisco Mus
eum of
Modern Art
Design Lec
ture Series
The Radical

'It is rare that perfect jobs fall into one's lap. I try to see the potential in a job, and gauge the willingness of a client to allow us to do our best work. The most important person to be tough and demanding with is oneself, not the client'

Jennifer Morla

'I believe that if you have ideals, passion and the power to make things happen, it is not that difficult. There are always people in the world who want ideas but if you start with the belief that ideas exist within you, as long as it is being transmitted around the world in some way, work will come to you automatically. If you do not have ideas, passion or the power to put ideas into practice it will be almost impossible'

Shin Matsunaga

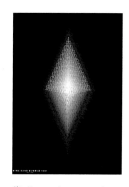

'I have always felt that too many designers compromise. It is my view that the design business will become more influential, and more profitable, if the designer becomes a genuine partner with his client and stands his ground. Most clients can easily detect weakness in presentation, therefore logic and commitment are essential parts of the client/designer relationship'

Michael Peters

'I don't think being tough or demanding is useful. It's important to be clear about what you want and be determined to get it. It's also important to ask for what you want and not leave it to other people's imagination. Remember most design groups are pretty unsophisticated about how they choose the people to build their Company's future with them. They're often poor at judging quality in people. I think designers find it easier to judge your work than to assess you. They'll see your past more clearly than your potential. I suggest that you prepare your answers to a key question that people will rarely ask, and be certain to answer it anyway in your discussion. The question: Why should I hire you?'

Michael Wolff

Shin Matsunaga's poster promoting the Nima Sand Museum, Japan
Below Michael Peters's symbol for Huhtamaki
Opposite Jennifer Morla's poster for the San Francisco Museum of Modern Art design lecture series 'The Radical Response' (Detail)

Q

When starting up your business for the first time, how do you go about getting customers?

'It is different for different people. I recommend going on interviews with clients that you want to work for. It should be what you want to do because you just might get the work. Exposure is how you will get work. One effective way of getting exposure is to do work for non-profit or design organisations. For example, announcements for the ballet, graphic design exhibitions, etc. Any organisation with high visibility. Think of every piece you do as your last promotion piece. Good work gets more work'

Michael Vanderbyl

'Through friends and by offering your services for free to clients who will let you do your best. Remember, you are building up your credentials!'

Massimo Vignelli

'In the hugely competitive UK packaging market it was extremely important for us to have a business point of difference, as our potential clients viewed most of our competitors as being 'creative'. Creativity was therefore the point of view, not the point of difference. Once we had established our point of difference we decided to pursue the kind of client we wanted, rather than any old client who approached us. A friend advised us that 'clients will judge you by the company you keep' so it was important to us to develop relationships with client companies we felt would have the exciting brand design projects we wanted. We pursued them through a combination of letters, phone calls, advertising agency referrals and networking. Public relations (being seen in the press to have a point of view) was also enormously successful for us. Clients not only became aware of us but also understood a little of what we stood for. Once the first few clients were won this way, and our client list and creative work demonstrated the effectiveness of our point of difference, other clients were attracted to us. Word-of-mouth is the most powerful new business tool'

Mark Wickens

'Naive hope, mixed with incompetence'

John Warwicker

JERSEY UNDERSHIRT
PURE COTTON 🌳

Bhs

TRUNK
PURE COTTON 🌳

Bhs

SLIP
PURE COTTON 🌳

Bhs

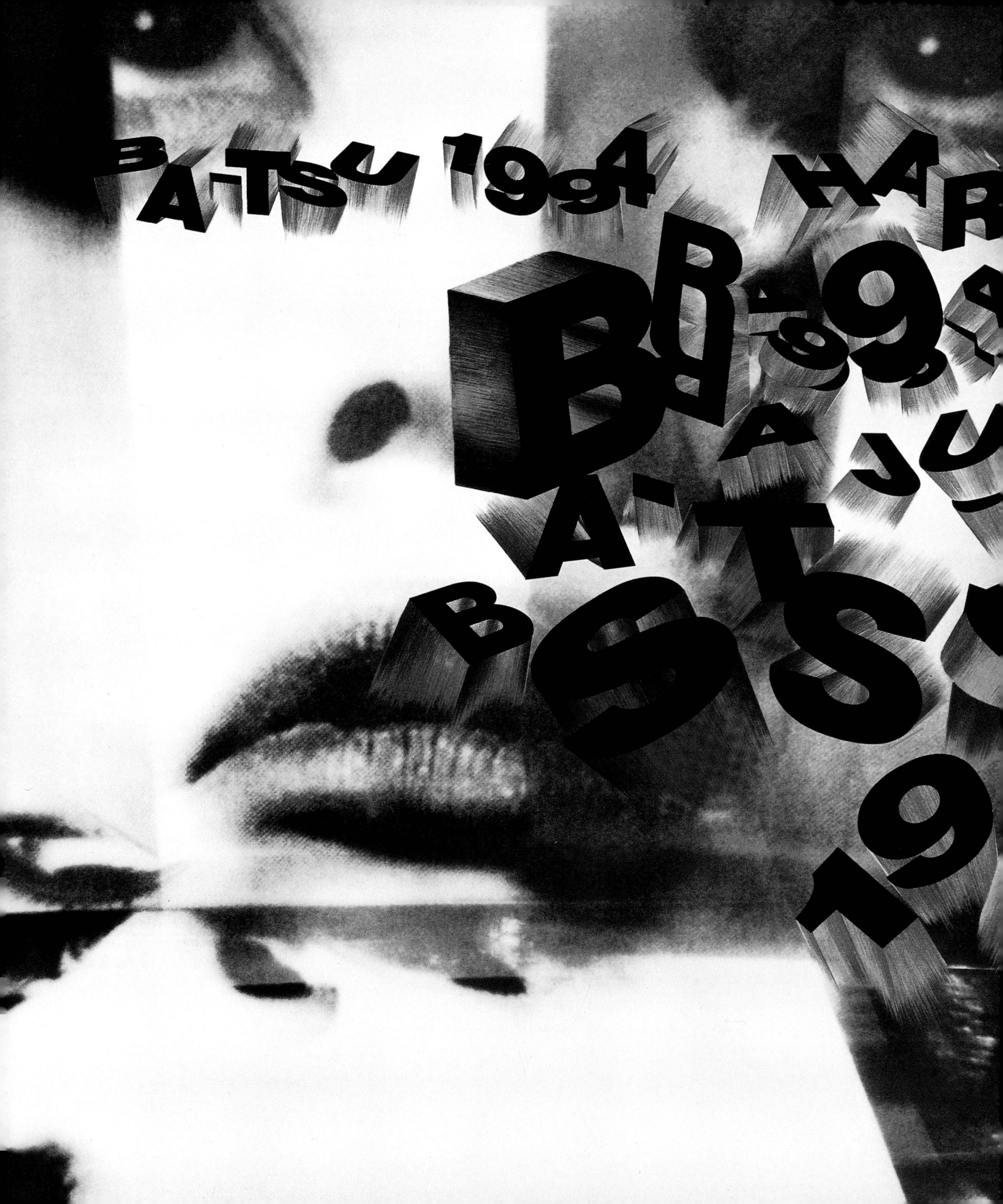
BA-TSU 1994 HAR

'My business was started in 1980.
I always try to meet the owner
of the company to get the job'
Makoto Saito

'Design practices don't start in a vacuum.
For everyone there is a small client
base even if sometimes they are relatives.
The best thing a potential client can I
say is 'I saw the job you did for so and
so. I thought it was really good. Now
I have this problem…' or 'I've heard
you're good at…' Moral: from day one
give even the smallest job your best,
do it well, understand the problem
in your client's terms, make sure the
people you want to work for have
heard of you, don't bore them'
Brian Sadgrove

'Send out a mailer to prospective clients.
Tell them that you exist, that you are
available, what your design philosophy
is, that you're competitive. Do some
work for relatives and friends (the worst
clients) and let them spread the word.
If you do a conscientious and good job
word will get around and you will build
a project portfolio'
Steff Geissbuhler

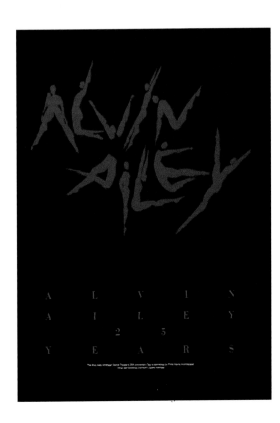

Brian Sadgrove's logotype for RIO,
a retail clothing range
Left Steff Geissbuhler's poster
promoting the 25th Anniversary Tour
of the Alvin Ailey Dance Theatre
Opposite Makoto Saito's poster for
Ba-Tsu, a fashion boutique (Detail)

'We started without needing to promote ourselves. It just happened that friends who started their own business asked us for advice about designing such things as identities and promotional pieces. It was mostly in the fashion world in the late 70's'

Jean Robert

'Draw attention to yourself in the marketplace by demonstrating your ability in an outstanding way. Your commitment, enthusiasm and capacity to produce better work than your competitors become your most effective marketing tools'

Garry Emery

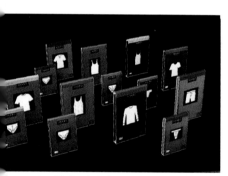

Jean Robert's packaging for
Hanro Liestal
Right Garry Emery's logotype for
the 10th Annual Melbourne Festival

'Practice what you believe in. Communicate in a way with people that makes your point and expresses your difference. Let them feel your passion for what you do and see the style that you've created for yourself. Before you start, make sure you know the answer to this question. What makes me/us different? Then let people know you're there. Write letters and call, and write postcards and call. Exist for them. Be creative for them. You are a brand. Get in their mind. Check what you write or what you're going to say with someone you respect. Make sure that you sound like you and not some nervous 'first time' letter writer. Most of all keep your enthusiasm high. Remember that 'no' usually means not now. Don't be concerned about rejection. The Reader's Digest isn't; it just keeps asking. So just keep writing simple letters that ask for a meeting and not a project. That comes later. It may take a hundred letters and phone calls to get one meeting but you only need one client with a project for you to

'Time, experience and the client's financial possibilities'

Massimo Vignelli

'Several factors. The perceived value of the work to the user, market value, hourly rates based on a defined scope of work and extent of services, the type of project (and nature of the client) and personal interest. All these play a part in formulating the cost of our work. Disbursements usually amount to 20% of the fees and are charged at cost'

Garry Emery

'I have two levels on which my pricing is based. The first level is a standard hourly rate multiplied by the hours I think it will take to complete the project, plus 10%. The second level is a lower hourly rate for jobs that will enable me to cross over into new areas. If I know a job will allow me to gain experience in a new work category, I'll prepare a lower bid for that job. For example, expanding from fashion to furniture. Never do speculative work. Ever'

Michael Vanderbyl

Michael Vanderbyl's interior design and plan for Robert Talbott, a New York menswear retailers

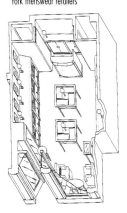

'The prices are set according to an established budget'

Makoto Saito

'Our prices are based upon
1 Cumulative knowledge of costs of similar projects/programs and educated guesses. Estimates by phases eg: pre-design/analysis/conceptual Sometimes, prices are set phase by phase. So in big projects, later phases are estimated during earlier phases of work. Design development, production, pre-press, documentation, supervision/observation of fabrication/printing.
2 Clues + cues from clients
3 Expenses
General Expenses: reimbursable expenses are defined below: We used to, and still hope to, get a mark up Communication (telephone, telex and telefax), shipping (air and ground), messenger services, packing, postage and freight. Reproduction costs to include blueprints, stats, photocopies, laser prints, film and processing, photo prints, acetate colour overlays and transfer proofs. Materials to include computer disks, art supplies, graphic materials, model materials and photographic materials. Special buy-outs to include typography and photo use fees.
4 A sense of what is right'

Deborah Sussman

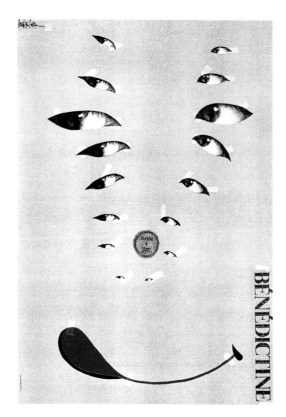

'I think what Pentagram would charge.

Then I cut it in half'

Bob Gill

'I base my prices on a mixture of four things. What I think my work will be worth to my clients based on my assessment of what it will achieve for them. By this criteria I can never charge enough! What I think they will expect to pay in the current competitive design market. By this criteria I will probably be so anxious to win the job that I'll always charge too little! What I'm prepared to do the work for in the circumstances that I'm at the time. Usually overdrawn. What I feel is right. This comes last and it's usually accurate. An intelligent and confident client doesn't buy creativity on price. To be really useful to each other, you and your client will need a relationship based on trust and mutual respect'

Michael Wolff

'There are various methods available. My own considerations include the contemplation and expression applied by the artist, evaluations of the work by others, the significance and influence of the work in a social context, and the value-added content in proportion to how frequently it is viewed by the public. Whichever way you look at it, the fluctuation in price is not determined by the negotiation process (even though there are cases like this). In the end, I think the price is objectively set in accordance to the work. My honest opinion is that there are no set rules and that the value of each work will always differ'

Shin Matsunaga

Shin Matsunaga's poster for the Japan Graphic Designers Association entitled 'I'm Here'

Q

If there was an alternative profession you could have entered what would it be? If there isn't one, why?

'A counterfeiter. I have the skills to be a very successful one. Recognition is something else; I don't like the implications of becoming a famous counterfeiter'

Henry Steiner

Shin Matsunaga's poster for the Tokyo Art Directors Club entitled 'From Tokyo'
Above Henry Steiner's banknote designs for the Standard Chartered Bank
Opposite Vaughan Oliver's 'A Very Modern Calendar' designed with Chris Bigg for V23 (detail)

'I am glad that designing exists as a profession. However I don't think this question is very appropriate for me. I have not thought about it before. If there was another area that I felt was appropriate it would be a multi-skilled athlete. I am not saying that I think I am a super fit sportsman. I would like to become an athlete because I feel that it involves a 'fairness of spirit' that I also adhere to. However, to do this requires the ability to maintain strength and a balance between all areas of the sport. In this age of specialists, I am attracted to the ultimate amateurism of multi-skilled athletics. That is also because even in the world of design I would like to be like that'

Shin Matsunaga

'As a teenager I loved football. I captained my school and district teams, was selected at county level and went on to represent my college in the finals of a national competition. I knew a lot more about Pele and George Bass than I did about Milton Glaser but I also knew that I could never make it at a professional level. When my college tutor demanded I choose between drawing board and turf the former seemed more sensible. In fact at college I was more inspired by illustration than graphics. Illustration appeared to allow more freedom for personal expression and an outlet for one's imagination whereas the jargon of typography and the technicalities of the print process bogged me down. Eighteen months after leaving college however, I found myself working in Michael Peter's packaging design studio, more by default than aspiration. I realised that there were people to help with the practicalities of putting a job into print and I was able to operate with a fair degree of intuition. But I was also harbouring another obsession, music, and I believed that one day I'd find the opportunity to design one of those record sleeve things, even though my tutors warned me that it wasn't an occupation for a professional man'

Vaughan Oliver

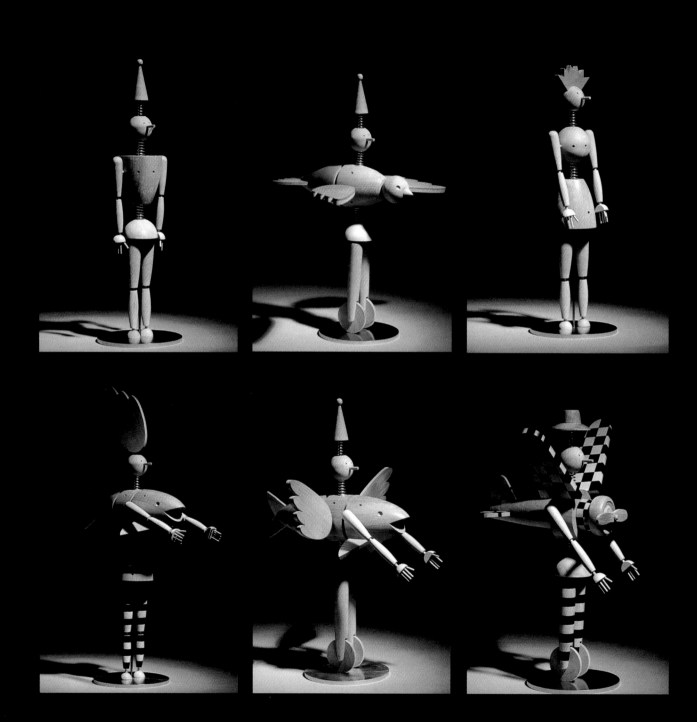

'I have always wanted to be a designer, though I also wanted to be an architect. Fortunately, I am now doing both'
Michael Vanderbyl

'Architecture would be my alternative profession. To be involved in designing a form to be built in context: landscape, streetscape, to use technology and materials appropriate to the time and be a space of protection, comfort, enjoyment and efficiency for the occupants. Graphic design is essentially ephemeral and it does respond to context; it reflects technology and can be useful/challenging to its users. As the discipline of design is increasingly understood, appreciated and accepted, incorporation by our communities will be far more reaching'
John Nowland

'Architecture'
Massimo Vignelli

'Conceptual video artist like Gary Hill or Bill Viola'
Jennifer Morla

'Up until the last few years I thought I would really like to be an architect. The built world interests me, and the nature of space and form is more fascinatingcthan surface. However, if I was to be an architect I would like to design better than I do as a graphic designer, and with a sounder philosophical base. As I get older I take some comfort in the ephemeral nature of graphics'
Brian Sadgrove

Below Brian Sadgrove's logotype for Koala, a manufacturer of spherical children's playground units
Opposite Michael Vanderbyl's toy design for George Belarian 'Toys By Artists', created to help children understand the concept of Surrealism

'I have never given much thought to it. Now that you are asking, it has to be a design-driven profession such as fashion designer, architect, photographer or anything related to art and design, which is where my interest lies. I would also like to be the owner of an antique shop or contemporary Chinese tea house since these are my favourite hobbies'
Alan Chan

'In ascending order of preference, I would have liked to have practiced stage design, architecture, history and then poetry. In any case, I wanted to seek and/or create symbols and attempt to console our lives. But even though I was very serious when I was seventeen I was not Arthur Rimbaud and I chose to become a graphic designer'
Pierre Bernard

Alan Chan's packaging for Mr Chan Tea Rooms
Right Pierre Bernard's publication for the French National Parks Ministry of Environment, designed with Dirk Behage and Fokke Draaijer
Opposite Pierre Bernard's symbol for the French National Parks Ministry of Environment, designed with Dirk Behage and Fokke Draaijer (Detail from poster)

'There were all sorts of alternative professions to choose. From Anthropologist, that's what I really wish I'd wanted to be, to Zoologist. I would have liked to have been a writer. Maybe I can change what I'm doing. Anyway I never chose design, I escaped into it'
Michael Wolff

I don't know where I'm going but I'm on my way

'The best place in the world for you to study graphics is right where you are. Your intention to become a designer and your ability to see what everything looks like and 'says' are the keys to your own personal course. You are the most critical part of any course you take. The people who teach you can only inspire you and draw your talent out. Of course some teachers may be more skilled than others and some colleges more stimulating and better equipped than others. The grass will always be greener somewhere else. Some countries will have well-developed design industries and some places may need designers to help them develop their countries. I don't believe there is anywhere that a good designer won't find a way of being useful. If you're going to be good at designing you'll never stop studying so it will always be a good idea to travel or even live and work for a while in many cultures and learn from everything everywhere'

Michael Wolff

Q

Which do you think is the best place in the world to study graphic design? The country of the most influence? The college of the most influence?

'Any place. Japan. None'

Takenobu Igarashi

Left Takenobu Igarashi's aluminium sculpture for the Kajima Corporation
Opposite Alan Fletcher's poster for the ICOGRADA Student Seminar (Detail)

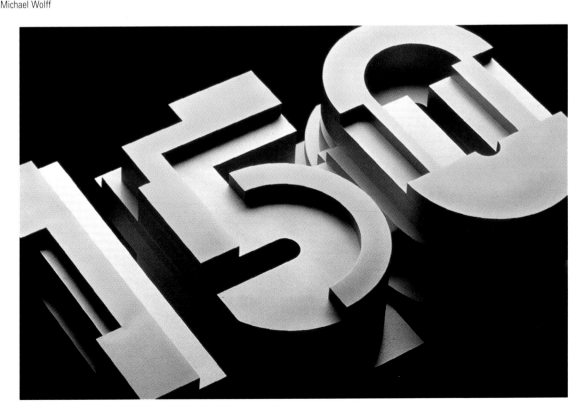

'Your own head has to be the best place to study graphic design. Like weather patterns on the planet, places change. Many influences come from many different places. One country's influence can and will change. I'll stick my neck out and say the countries with the most influence are: Japan, Holland, UK, Italy and USA. It seems to be collective. The next influences: Russia, Asia and Australia? The colleges of the most influence: School of Visual Arts, New York; and the Royal College of Art, UK'

David Lancashire

'USA: it combines European theory with capitalist opportunities. Holland: solid history in design education and a liberal attitude toward eclectic styling. Switzerland: brain-numbing training into rigid discipline. Germany (some places): there is a trend towards integration of design disciplines such as product design, communication design, interior design and interface design. Design is taught as an integrated process, performed in teams and not dominated by individualistic artistic expression'

Erik Spiekermann

David Lancashire's logotype
for Cicada Press
Right Tibor Kalman's magazine
layout for 'Colors'
Opposite John Warwicker's video
designed with Tomato

J AN CHEN: In China, it's very important for a woman, no matter how old she is, to always appear innocent.

'Zimbabwe. The possibilities are wide open, you could teach yourself'

Tibor Kalman

'Best place in the world to study graphic design: Basel, Switzerland; country of most influence: (New York) USA; and the college of the most influence: University of Cincinnati, USA'

Massimo Vignelli

'Where you are at the moment'

John Warwicker

Years ago
I was an
angry young man
I'd pretend
that I was a billboard
Standing tall

The basic attitude towards design 'The dot with its cosmic infinity; the line extending like a metaphor of life; the grid holding infinite possibility in its units; the plane created through lines and shades; forms like circles, triangles, squares and letters; and the light reflected from the surface of an object perceived in the eye as colour. These are the things that I work with. To put it concretely, in my design I aim for simple composition using strong and universal forms. Moreover, attitudes such as serenity, joy or warmth add to its perfection'

Takenobu Igarashi

My Design Philosophy
Each project must be carefully analysed
and its individuality articulated; the
solution needs to be appropriate to its
client. If I don't decide where I'm going
beforehand, I won't know when I arrive.
Visual subjectivity is more appropriate
to certain categories (eg posters) than
to others (eg annual reports); corporate
work should look more objective.
I consider 'style' irrelevant and take
conscious pains to expunge it (and
especially the latest trend) from my work;
personality, however, is inescapable and
will appear involuntarily. The optically
seductive aspect of design is vital, but
for me the conceptual takes precedence.
Contrast, whether visual or psychological,
is essential in enlivening a design.
I consciously try to incorporate elements
of the Chinese and Asian vocabulary in
my work; this helps make it distinctive
and it is appropriate to my environment.
Designers should not be ashamed to
demonstrate intelligence and culture in
their work. Against visual pollution, the
designer's mind, eye and hand are their
best weapons'

Henry Steiner

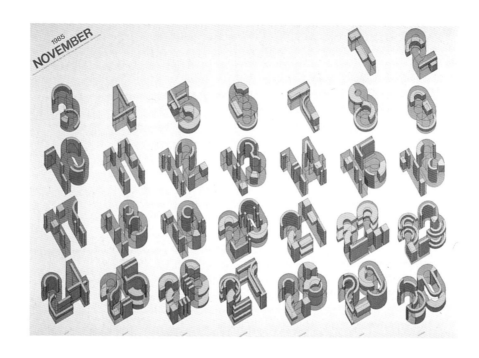

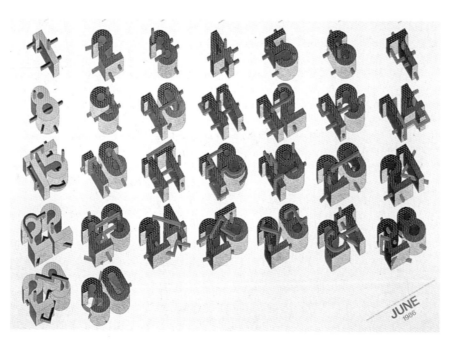

'The future of computing and computers isn't easy to imagine. But when keyboards and computers can listen and react intelligently, computers will become less 'separate'. I think they will take their place with other colleagues and other means of self expression'

Michael Wolff

'The computer is today, and tomorrow will continue to be, the operational tool of our profession and we have to use it to express our ideas. The other methods are obsolete'

Massimo Vignelli

People now believe the future of design lies in marrying ideas with the computer. Can you see there will always be a niche for designers who choose to create with other mediums?

Opposite Takenobu Igarashi's poster-sized calendar for the Museum of Modern Art, New York

Yes

Takenobu Igarashi

'Computers are convenient machines but humans have a visual sense that stems from the heart. Designing from the human computer is marvellous. However, this is feasible only for those with the talent to create. It is necessary to constantly refine the creative sensibility acquired prior to mastering the computer. By this, I mean the study from your student years. In particular, gaining the ability to study objects and then express oneself is important'

Shigeo Fukuda

'Idea first and foremost every time; everything follows thereafter! Without the idea in the first instance, the computer is a waste of time. Young people must think first! I have seen too many young people sit down in front of a computer and expect an idea to somehow suddenly appear before them on the computer screen. That is not the way it happens! I believe there will always be a 'niche' for designers to create in other mediums, to create with pencil, pen, brush or scissors. To work together with craftspeople to create metal or timber pieces of all formats is a fulfilling process and will never die. The computer is a useful tool to produce design work solutions after an idea is conceived. It is not the only way and never will be!'

Barrie Tucker

Shigeo Fukuda's poster for The First
Paper Works Grand Prix 1991
Right Barrie Tucker's packaging for
Tulloch 100th Anniversary Tawny Port

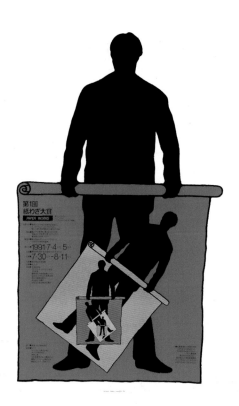

'The question reveals a certain kind of fuzzy-headed anxiety about the changes we are going through technically, aesthetically and ethically because of the computer. The value system is changing at an enormous rate but the questions of a designer's niche outside of the computer is misplaced. Essentially, designers are paid to think. The computer may or may not be an aid to this process'

Milton Glaser

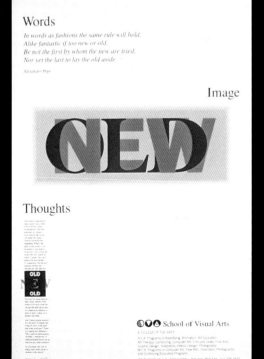

'What do you mean by design? Get rid of the word. It is meaningless. You respond to a situation and produce work. You choose the craft by which you articulate that work. 'Design' doesn't come into it. This is not against intelligence, just method. Over the last 30 years or so 'design' has set up models for working that are not only incredibly prescriptive and totally restrictive but also artificial and increasingly redundant. They deny so much. These models are perpetuated by the educational establishments and by those who feel there is an industry. There isn't an industry out there. Just work, live and enjoy'

John Warwicker

Sixteenth century England was a time of great industry and imagination in everything from shipbuilding to playwriting and map-making.

The cartographer *Christopher Saxton* is less well known than William Shakespeare or Henry VIII, but he was the father of map-making in England.

While Shakespeare mapped the human spirit, *Saxton* mapped the world.

Having surveyed 34 English countries between 1574 and 1579, *Saxton's* were the first maps in which English towns and villages could be identified.

Through the century, *Saxton's* maps were of great use in the defence of England against the French invasion forces and the Spanish Armada.

Saxton's maps were engraved on copper plates by the finest craftsmen and printed, some hand coloured, on the finest papers of the day.

Today the maps are as bright and detailed as they were over 400 years ago.

'Yes, you can marry ideas with computers. As a tool they're great but can they think? A good idea is a good idea, is it not? The opportunity to have a deluge of mindless rubbish is greater now than ever before. The niche will always be there for people who choose other media, it is in our psyche. They said when videos came out it would kill off cinemas. This has not happened. Will the computer kill the book?'

David Lancashire

David Lancashire's poster for Australian Paper promoting Saxton stock

Q

How will the print medium be affected by computer generated mediums, such as the Internet, VR and multimedia?

'God only knows, but I doubt whether he cares! Paper will be reference material not a storage material; computers will distribute and store information. For true pleasure and physical enjoyment we'll use paper. We won't ship magazines or newspapers across the globe as much as we do now, instead we'll print them out locally, maybe even at home'

Erik Spiekermann

'There has been considerable change over the past few years and we all see to what extent our communities embrace technology. There will also be demand for printed items either traditionally or from a printer, a small personal colour one, beside our computer printing out specific files from the Internet or multimedia. What designers must not forget is who we are designing for, how we can best communicate to that audience, whether via the Internet, CD-ROM, or full colour or single colour print. Design to the medium, for the audience'

John Nowland

Erik Spiekermann's font 'Officina' for the International Typeface Corporation
Opposite John Warwicker's stills from a video designed with Tomato

'As most of the modern media is additional rather than replacement technology, print will survive and flourish. The real question is whether there is enough sustainable forest to cope with the proliferation of print?'

John Warwicker

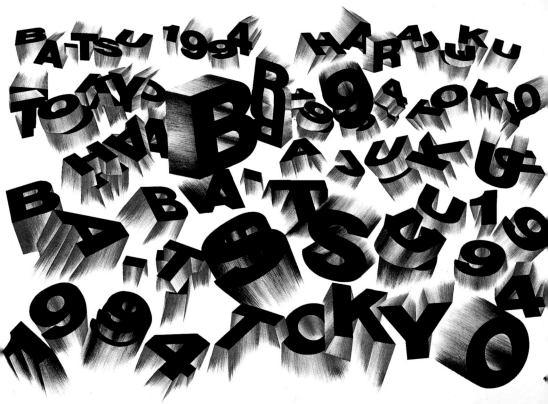

'Minuteness increases, and work speed also increases. However, I feel something is lacking because I cannot believe that I am creating it'

Makoto Saito

'The question should be: How soon will the electronic media be affected by print? When 'computer art' was first launched it was as primitive as the first silent movies. Truly far out stuff like the map of Africa morphing to a Coke bottle! In those days I could smell work done on computers and I didn't like the aroma. Then, about ten years ago, the machines got more sophisticated and when there was a demonstration of a computer generated design on the screen which had my 'handwriting', I was sold. I didn't become converted to the boxes, they evolved to my standards.

If it wasn't for print (and cinema) the boxes today wouldn't be delivering subtle colours, finer detail, flatter screens, nuanced and historically accurate typography; they'd still be klutzy machines run by gee-whiz nerds. Technology has always been a refuge for the creatively challenged. Progress consists of making the craft more transparent. The distance from inspiration to realisation is always diminishing.

In the meantime, print is benefiting from better typography (thanks to people like Adobe), layering and unusual combinations of images, the ability (thanks to Photoshop) of adjusting pictures closer to one's original concept. Viewing designs first on the screen has given us a greater tolerance for rough images on paper. At the same time (thanks to electronics and stochastic techniques, for example) print is becoming ever finer, more accurate and capable of grace'

Henry Steiner

Henry Steiner's poster promoting the play 'The Joy Luck Club' for Northern Telecom Asia/Pacific
Opposite Makoto Saito's poster for Ba-Tsu, a fashion boutique

'Hopefully, because there are more and more alternative media, print will improve its effectiveness. It will have to be better thought out, better looking and better written. It will have to feel wonderful'
Michael Wolff

'Too soon to say, but it could be bad'
Massimo Vignelli

'Technological breakthroughs, particularly in innovative computer systems and new software developments, have had a revolutionary effect on the print medium. These effects are not all bad; while such technology will reduce the number of designers working in the industry in the future, I believe that it will also lead to an improvement in the quality of the print medium'
Michael Peters

'For the immediate future, sensitive designers will remain in the tactile zone'

Vaughan Oliver

Massimo Vignelli's corporate identity and packaging for Galerias, a department store in Spain
Right Vaughan Oliver's poster promoting an album launch for Scheer
Opposite Michael Peter's literature system for National Power

Didcot

Coal-fired power station

Deeside

Combined cycle gas turbine

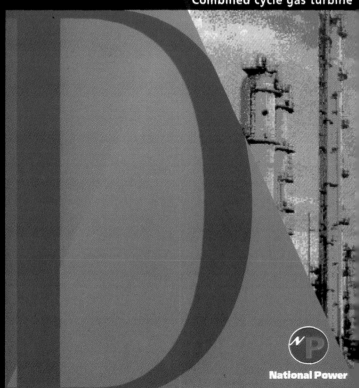

communication
communica

mmunica
ommunicat

'The protection of intellectual property and its manifestations has been made virtually untenable by the introduction of electronic media. The laws (in the UK) are completely inadequate, basically because the physical criteria is so narrow that small adjustments to a piece of work render it safe from being legislated against. Also the means of (electronic) distribution is invisible; it means that it is really hard to establish exact usage once you have handed over the disc'

John Warwicker

'Copyright will, I think, become more difficult to control. With the advent of computers and the onslaught of images that can be manipulated so quickly: under and overlaid, colourised and stretched and expanded, and then thrown out into the mobius strip of technology convergence. Take video clips, rock clips and so on, hundreds of different flickering images in front of you, in some cases for milliseconds. How do you control this?'

David Lancashire

'At the beginning of the design process we make it clear to our clients that the designs presented remain under copyright until we have formally assigned copyright to them. Copyright is assigned to the client shortly after they formally approve the designs, so that it can be registered in their names. They then own the design and we don't. Because of the commercial value placed on the ownership of a specific design, for instance a brand mark, most of our work is formally assigned to our clients. I have always been rather philosophical about the 'misapplication' of anything we have designed. It happens. But it seems to happen less where mutual trust exists. I have always assumed that our work will be eventually changed or replaced by the work of others'

Brian Sadgrove

Left David Lancashire's poster promoting the Warradjan Aboriginal Cultural Centre for the Australian Nature Conservation Agency
Opposite John Warwicker's stills from a video designed with Tomato
Below Brian Sadgrove's logotype for Arts Victoria

ARTS VICTORIA

'To the best of my knowledge, one cannot copyright an idea. Prevention is the best protection. Hire a good contract attorney to detail your usage rights and put them on all contracts so as to prevent misuse and promote a clear understanding of who owns what'

Jennifer Morla

'Always ask an expert. Legislation is constantly changing'

Michael Wolff

'It has always been impossible to legally protect an idea. The physical representation of that idea must be realised before any authorship can be proven. Today, this physical representation usually takes the shape of data, which in itself is invisible. As it is so easy to manipulate data without changing the visual appearance, protection of ideas, concepts and digital artwork has become more of a moral issue. Legally it is almost impossible to detect whether data is based on other data or whether it is based on an original concept. If you, for example, want to copy a typeface, you have two choices without getting caught:

1   You take the original data of the outline information and move all the points on a character by a few percent in one or two directions. This will corrupt the data but will hardly be evident on the output. It may become less well-behaved font in production but that seems to be of little concern to the font pirates

2   You scan a clean print of the original typeface, convert the scans to font outlines, attribute some character widths, and - bingo! - you've got yourself a new typeface. It's definitely worse than the original but you can make hundreds of copies and sell them a lot cheaper. My advice: never send open, unprotected data to anybody, not even your best friends. You never know who might get into their computer. If a client, however, has paid a licence fee for unlimited use of your artwork, font or whatever, they may have a right to use your original data. Always be clear about what you will supply, who is entitled to what, and never leave loose data around!'

Erik Spiekermann

Jennifer Morla's packaging for Apple Computers' Quicktime CD Digipack
Opposite Erik Spiekermann's font 'Officina' for the International Typeface Corporation

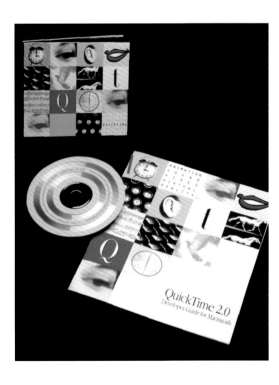

ITC Officina

ITC Officina was originally conceived as a typeface to bridge the gap between old fashioned typewriter type and a traditional typographic design. The design goal was to create a small family of type ideally suited to the tasks of office correspondence and business documentation.

Midway through the design, however, it became obvious that this face had capabilities far beyond its original intention. Production tests showed that ITC Officina could stand on its own as a highly legible and remarkably functional type style.

The European design team, under the close guidance of the Berlin designer, Erik Spiekermann, was given the directive to continue the work on ITC Officina, but now with two goals. The first was to maintain the original objective of the design: to create a practical and utilitarian tool for the office environment. And the second was to develop a family of type suitable to a wide range of typographic applications.

- a practical and utilitarian tool for the office environment

What developed is a different sort of type family. It has a distilled range of just two weights: Book and Bold (medium weight being unnecessary in office correspondence) with complementary Italics. In addition, ITC Officina is available in two styles: Serif and Sans. The end result is an exceptionally versatile communication tool packaged in a relatively small type family.

Proportionally, the design has been kept somewhat condensed to make the family space economical. Special care was also taken to insure that counters were full and serifs sufficiently strong to withstand the rigors of small sizes, modest resolution output devices, telefaxing, and less than ideal paper stock.

ITC Officina combines the honest "information only" look of a typewriter face with the benefits of better legibility, additional stylistic choices, and more economical use of space. We believe that it has admirably met both its design goals.

h h h h

The *italic* designs could have been rendered as simple oblique romans, but cursive overtones were incorporated to provide distinction and character.

to withstand

ITC Officina is available as a *serif* or *sans* serif design, in Book and Bold weights with corresponding Italics.

Alternate numbers have been drawn to provide additional flexibility of use.

serve the purpose of improving character legibility

Sans &Serif

serve the purpose of improving character legibility

'Traits like the left-pointing serif of the "i" and "j," the tail of the lowercase "l," and the slightly heavy punctuation, which link this design to its typewriter-like cousins, also serve the dual purpose of improving character legibility.

to withstand

- suitable to a wide range of typographic applications

- Only licensed ITC Subscribers and their sublicensees are authorized to reproduce, manufacture, and offer for sale the ITC typefaces shown in this issue.

'The question of how and if ideas can be copyrighted is a problem for the law and lawyers. While it is important to prevent your ideas from being copied by those who seek to exploit it for commercial reasons, it is equally significant to allow your ideas to enter the world. Sometimes it is difficult to distinguish which is more important. Computers have merely amplified the issue'

Milton Glaser

'Protection of intellectual property rights on the designs should be established prior to the computer age. As we are heading towards the 21st Century, it is inevitable that the client will ask for graphics on disc. Thus, in order to safeguard our own benefits, a well-written contract is necessary before the commencement of work. To me, there are only two ways to deal with client who has infringed the contract: either to seek legal action or never deal with the same client again'

Alan Chan

'Copyright of ideas never works. Good ideas belong to mankind, if you are not interested, stay out'

Massimo Vignelli

Opposite
Alan Chan's packaging for The Swank Shop, a fashion retailer

'One of the most influential elements that I incorporate into my work is 'culture'. Culture has always influenced art; it is so deeply rooted in every society that nothing can match its importance. Culture is not only a link to tradition and history, it also provides the essence of all vital conceptual and visual elements. In capturing the spirit of culture and expressing it through one's own unique design execution, its potential becomes boundless and timeless. It is my ambition that, through weaving culture into commercial design, I can create work that would inject energy and life into our everyday lives. By doing so, appreciation of design may transcend generations and nationalities, and touch people in all corners of the world. As a designer working primarily in the East, I am able to combine two cultures, often breaking new ground for Asian design. I create my contemporary Oriental style by the fusion of eastern and western cultural elements, in a nostalgic and contemporary, modern and classic manner'

Alan Chan's packaging for Chungking's
Chinese Cake Shop

Q

'I really can't

Everywhere one looks/everywhere one goes/every aspect of contemporary life from personal to civic to commercial - utilises graphic communication. So why be concerned about the future?

The reason is, that the danger is not to graphic design, it is to graphic designers! Unfortunately, I can imagine a global society without them. The practice is available to just about anyone who can handle the tools - and how many people can tell the difference between useful and stylish; let alone great!?

An apt counsel to the young can be found in Plato ca. 427-347 BC: 'The Punishment which the wise suffer, who refuse to take part in the government, is to live under the government of worse men'. My point is, that in order to obtain and maintain the clout that designers need and deserve - they must re-enforce each other and the profession; the must 'take part' in policy making and 'take on' the policy makers'

Deborah Sussman

Deborah Sussman's packaging for Pororoca products which formed part of a total retail concept for MYCAL Engineering
Right Alan Fletcher's poster promoting the G&B Arts Exhibition, a retrospective featuring 100 posters

Alan Fletcher

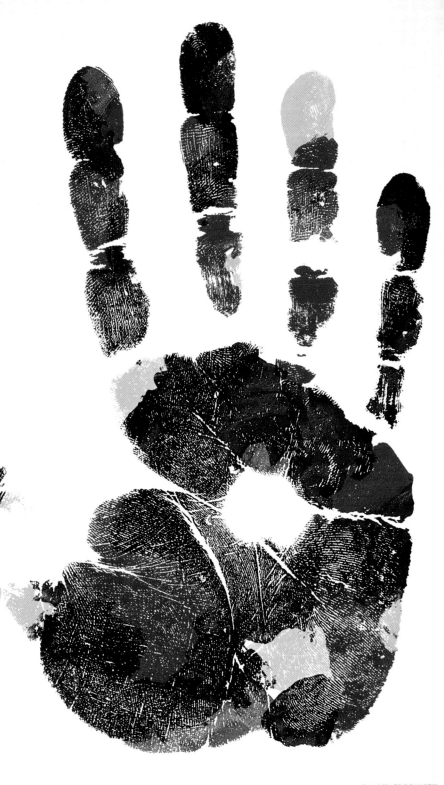

An exhibition
of 100 screen
printed posters

20th August to the
31st October 1993
Open every day
10.30am to 5.30pm
Admission £3.50
Concessions £2.50

The Design Museum
Butlers Wharf
London SE1 2YD
*South of the River
by Tower Bridge*

Underground:
*Tower Hill Station
London Bridge Station*
Docklands Light Railway:
Tower Gateway Station
British Rail:
London Bridge Station

Ample Parking:
*Note Tower Bridge is
closed to traffic during
August to October*

G&B Arts
at the
Design
Museum

A retrospective 1959 – 1993

Posters by:

Peter Blake
Patrick Caulfield
Peter Dixon
Max Ernst
Alan Fletcher
Abram Games
Brian Grimwood
John Heartfield
FHK Henrion
Howard Hodgkin
Gordon House
Allen Jones
Peter Kennard
George Mayhew
Tony Meeuwissen
John McConnell
Sarah Moon
Claus Oldenberg
Eduardo Paolozzi
Tom Phillips
John Piper
Ian Pollock
Bridget Riley
William Roberts
Maurice Sendak
Gerald Scarfe
Snowdon
Ralph Steadman
Barry Zaid
and others

GB

'No problem. We'd have more trees, more oxygen and about the same amount of confusion. Just a little less bullshit, because 92.587% of graphic design is bullshit, isn't it? Just a way of distorting information in service of commerce'

Tibor Kalman

'There's almost no graphic design in our society. It's all commercial art'

Bob Gill

Bob Gill's illustration for 'Fortune Magazine' entitled 'Traffic'

'I can't imagine one. Graphic images have always been there and they always will be there. Some 'graphic designer' has always created them. Look at the brilliance of pre-historic illustration'

Michael Wolff

'The need for visual communication is irreversible, therefore it should be good, responsible and beautiful'

Massimo Vignelli

'Humans have been creating marks for thousands of years. In its purest form design has wit, passion and sparks of genius. Add art to design and the work produced, I believe, has real integrity. Although I think the process has been more or less the same, the description has changed over time: commercial art, graphic design… communication consultants? Maybe we should drop marketing and add art. It seems that marketing has had the effect of producing wallpaper. Design under other names has been going on for centuries and will continue to do so. The question 'What effect has marketing had on the design process?' has to be asked'

David Lancashire

MARITIME MUSEUM OF VICTORIA

David Lancashire's logotype for the Maritime Museum of Victoria for Tony Geeves & Associates

Opposite Makoto Saito's posters promoting an exhibition 'The Cross', for the client Taiyo Printing Company Ltd

'I cannot envisage it'

Makoto Saito

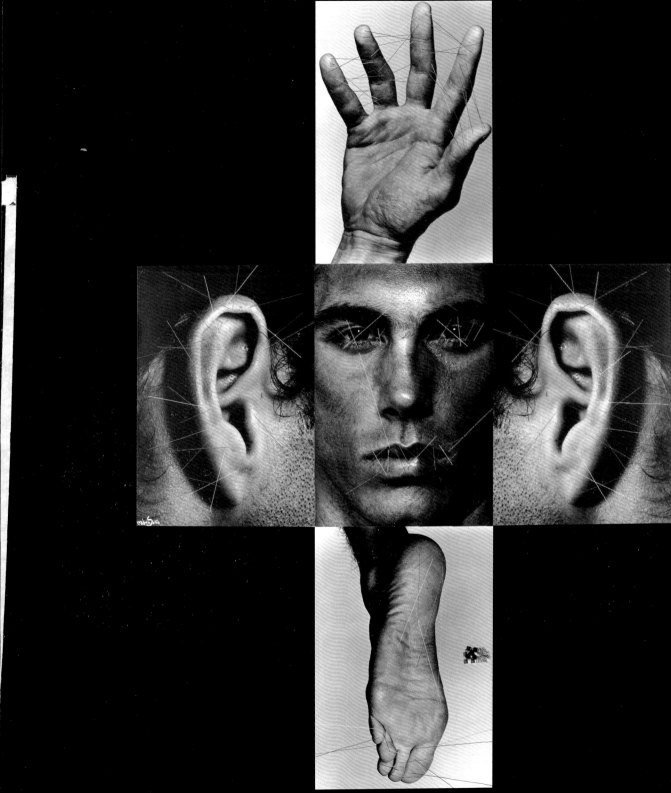

'Design philosophy is based on its own theory of design and how it interacts with the market and industry'

Massimo Vignelli

'Design has no philosophy. People who design have philosophies or stances about what they want to achieve by design. They have thoughts and attitudes about what being a designer can achieve for them, what it can achieve for their clients, and, sadly less often, what it can achieve for the world in general. In my case, I have never stuck to one view of what is good in design. For me design is a means by which any organisation of any size can maximise its effectiveness by engaging as fully as possible with people's emotions, their sensuality and their intellect. My personal goals have always remained the same: to enable organisations to express themselves in their own particular way for the benefit of anyone they're involved with, including themselves, and to do this in a way that brings value to everyone, to the rest of nature, to this planet we all share, and its future'

Michael Wolff

Q

Is the philosophy of design reflecting the demands of our environment such as the marketplace, or is it a reflection or response from the design profession?

Opposite Massimo Vignelli's packaging for Fassati Wines Erik Spiekermann's transport network map for BVG, Berlin Transportation Company

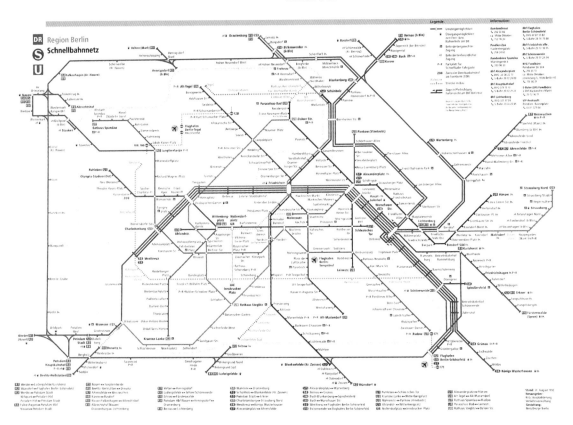

'Our work is not about the visual form as an end to itself; it is about the free space gained at the end of an intellectual and creative process, which results in concepts taking on different visual manifestations, depending on the influence of existing conditions and prevailing intentions'

Erik Spiekermann

'In all its work Chermayeff & Geismar is guided by the same basic philosophy: design is the solution to problems, rather than the arbitrary application of fashionable styles. Design solutions are derived from the careful analysis of each project's special needs'

Steff Geissbuhler

'Your work is the map of your experience'

John Warwicker

John Warwicker's stills from a video designed with Tomato

'The design industry is a double-edged sword. It has all the potential to feed off itself. Have we killed romanticism? Is Shakespeare really dead? For me, Michael Wolff's talk in Singapore 'Bursting the Designer Bubble' says it all; it had a profound effect on me. I hope he doesn't mind me stating this!'

David Lancashire

0024

D.C.–&A.C. SWITCH RANGES. CUT-OUT D.C.+&A.C. COMMON TERMINAL

INS. Ω×100 50 μA RESIST-ANCE
2·5V. Ω÷100 250 μA
10V. L.R. 10V. 1mA.
25V. 25V. 10mA.
100V. 1A. 100V. 100mA.
250V. 2·5A. 250V. 1A.
1000V. 10A. 500V. 10A.
D.C. 1000V. A.C.

MK III 8
A.C. & Ω RANGES REV M.C. D.C. RANGES

UNIVERSAL AVOMETER

ZERO Ω×100 ZERO Ω

ZERO Ω÷100

AC&DC. Dbs.
DECIBELS
CURRENT & VOLTAGE
RESISTANCE

2500V. A.C.   2500V. D.C.+

'Swiss industries are generally very conscious of the environment and ecological concerns. As a graphic designer I support the reduction of all print materials! I try to apply the thought of Mies van der Rohe 'Less is more"

Jean Robert

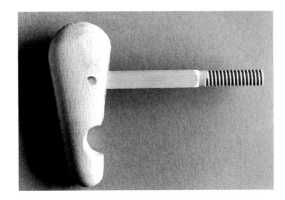

'For me it is reflecting the demands of the environment around us. As a commercial designer, my mission is to provide and create a design solution for my clients in order to get a share in a highly competitive marketplace. Our work has always reflected the everyday living environment, particularly Asia, where we have a similar culture'

Alan Chan

Jean Robert's photographic designs for 'Face to Face' (Lars Muller Publishers) designed in conjunction with Kati Durrer

'When did I fall in love with words and symbols on buildings and graphic images on the streets and rail lines that connected them? Perhaps it was as a child, riding the subways from Brooklyn to New York and seeing landmarks appear after emerging from the underground of DeKalb Avenue and downtown Brooklyn. Signs like 'SQUIBB' appeared, as though the toothpaste tube had grown gigantic and attached itself to the tower; or the mystifying and frightening board 'BELIEVE IN THE LORD JESUS CHRIST AND THOU SHALT BE SAVED' that announced one's arrival on the bridge over the East River. When the train descended underground again there was a series of stations with evocative names like Canal Street or Cortlandt Street suggesting other times and the early Dutch settlers whose lives helped shape the city. These names were rendered in tile and were knitted into the subway walls with patterns and mosaics that seemed inevitable and eternal, and in retrospect 'civic'. The graphics of New York's subway provided a system of clues that helped frame the experience of travelling from my family and its homogeneous residential core, to the great hub of the city. Many signals performed their public choreography, culminating in little red and green light bulbs overhead that marked the pedestrian routes along the turmoil of the 42nd street underground.

Later I got to travel across the US by railroad where the signals and signs along the tracks - as well as those hanging under spirited and welcoming station canopies - identified the lines on the exotic cross-country routes. Even little detailed messages inside the nobly furnished compartments, added up to a visual culture filled with suggestion, memory, anticipation, discovery and delight'

Deborah Sussman

'Holland: everything is designed but it's still a nice place. Also Zimbabwe'

Tibor Kalman

Q

We know that design is a powerful tool. Which country and its people do you think are the most 'affected' by design?

Deborah Sussman's logo and basketball court floor for the Cleveland Caveliers
Left Tibor Kalman's layout for 'Colors'

Every day we turn 11,000,000,000 kilos of perfectly good stuff into *Garbage* And some of us have actually figured out what to **DO** with it.

Todos los días convertimos 11.000.000.000 de kilos de cosas buenas en *Basura* Algunos ya sabemos qué **HACER** con ella.

COLORS 5

'Design has a powerful, integrating effect on the ordinary day-to-day lives of people in various cultures, often maintaining the strong traditional ties that can be seen in Bali, New Guinea, or in traditional Australian Aboriginal communities. Design plays an enormous part in the lives of these people. But we are more likely to link the idea of 'design' to places such as Scandinavia, Italy or Japan. Denmark and Finland are small, close-knit societies steeped in what can be called 'good design' cultures. They provide designers around the world with potent lessons and exemplars, being typically renowned for their fabrics, flatware, glassware, furniture and architecture. These elegant, distinctive cultures have no trouble continually renewing and reinventing themselves through design, while maintaining their identities. Similarly, Italian culture is heavily oriented towards design. The worldwide influence of Italian design has been a phenomenon at least since English architects in the 18th century began touring Italy's major neo-classical sites and returning home with Italian ideas. Today, so many of our contemporary notions of good design are defined and generated by Italian designers operating across a wide field of design areas, notably architecture, fashion, furniture, lighting, fabrics, motor cars and kitchenware. 'Japan is another example of a country in which design has a high profile. Traditional Japan has produced a rare degree of design purity and sophistication that impinges on the daily lives of virtually all Japanese. Europeans have been fascinated by this design culture for hundreds of years but now Japan's design reputation is built on its new aggressive approach to design, synthesising and transforming design references from different sources and cultures to create bold new design forms. In architecture, fashion, industrial design and graphic design, the Japanese demonstrate a fearless approach to novelty, and a lack of constraint absent from design traditions. This reflects an increasingly eclectic society that is consciously shedding old ways and experimenting with new forms Other countries too have recognised design strengths: Spanish architecture and engineering; German industrial design; Dutch typography; but it would be difficult to say that their peoples are widely affected by design. Perhaps that really still only occurs among traditional societies where lives are circumscribed by ritual and custom, and where design is an integral element of cultural expression in daily life'

Garry Emery

'Those who are contributing to this book and those who are reading it'

John Warwicker

'Germany'

Takenobu Igarashi

Alan Fletcher

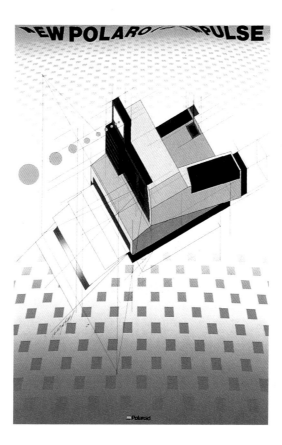

Takenobu Igarashi's poster
for the Polaroid Corporation

VOLLEYBAL

NEDERLAND

ROEIEN ROEIEN

NEDERLAND

80 c

NEDERLAND

VELDHOCKEY

NEDERLAND

80 c

80 c

80 c

80 c

ATLETIEK

SCHAATSEN

Steun onze olympische sporters
Koop en verzamel de
olympische wenskaarten

'Every country is affected by design because everything that God didn't make was made by a designer. Perhaps he or she didn't know they were acting as a designer but everything ever made by a person is the result of at least some design decision. The question is probably aimed at a perceived design culture in the modern, academic sense. There are countries with the deepest cultural roots that are the most influenced. Italy has an uninterrupted tradition of art and architecture and you can see it in the way even tractor drivers dress for work. Holland has a long democratic tradition in public design, and that's why even government forms look good there. The USA has a long history of destroying what was there before white people arrived, and they carry on with an amazing disregard for the visual environment. I could carry on but I don't want to reaffirm national stereotypes'

Erik Spiekermann

'For this question I looked up the meaning of 'design' in the dictionary. 'Be a designer: conceive mental plan for, construct the groundwork for a plot of - to have faculty of evolving general idea, construction, invention.' A country that provides consistent opportunity and encouragement for the application of design, either architectural, engineering or graphic design, and where design becomes a part of people's lives would be Denmark, Holland or Switzerland. I couch this observation not from having lived there but from the impressions of a visitor. I also believe that the size of these countries, and consistency and quality, as well as education, industry and government have considerable influence on design'

John Nowland

Massimo Vignelli's graphics program for COSMIT (Comitato Organizzatore Salone del Mobile Italiano), a trade fair organisation
Opposite Erik Spiekermann's stamp design for PTT Netherlands

'Denmark, for example. It has a very effective 'Design Centre' that helps industry, and the private and public sectors to improve design and achieve a better environment. A very civilised country indeed'

Massimo Vignelli

'Every individual, even people who are blind, is affected by perceptions of appearance. It's an integral part of being alive. Different cultures have different ways of noticing and ordering the various meanings communicated by appearance in every aspect of life. Everyone, everywhere is affected by the results of design'

Michael Wolff

Q

Do you think that society generally has a good understanding of what graphic design is? How can we improve society's views on graphic design and graphic designers?

'There is not a clear idea of what a graphic designer is. Do you wonder why? Look around. We are getting what we deserve'

Massimo Vignelli

'It depends which society you're concerned about. For example, in Switzerland you don't have to explain what a graphic designer is and does, where as in the US you still do. Society by itself has no view about graphic design, or it's as much as you know about insurance, physics or brain surgery. Society does not have to know about graphic design in order to survive. The only thing we can all do in educating our clients is to explain our work and thought processes, and let them play a part in solving the problem. In other words, society does not have to know about graphic design as long as it understands that we are communication professionals who can solve problems. You don't have to know anything about law when you seek a lawyer to solve a legal problem. You don't hear doctors complain that their patients don't know anything about medicine, or that they have to educate society before the cure can be effective'

Steff Geissbuhler

'Although there may be a growing awareness of graphic design in Australian society, I feel it has mainly come about through publicity developed by high profile designers and their specific projects of public interest.
'I believe that there must be more of an educational promotional campaign developed through travelling exhibitions (featuring all types of graphic design) to be viewed by the public throughout the country. Sponsorship for such events is required but it should be an aim of AGDA in Australia to make this happen. The AGDA Awards exhibition should also be seen by society in general and not simply put on show for designers only! 'Graphic designers should stop being so private, elitist and, in many instances, self-conscious, and they should become more public. We should be proud to show our design to the people - show and explain to the general public what we do; to demonstrate the role we play in the everyday life of the nation. A 'show and tell' on a public scale'

Barrie Tucker

'No, but as a profession we are not alone. By being united and supportive of the industry, and by consistently performing in the delivery of quality, intelligent and appropriate solutions, the acceptance, understanding and reputation of our profession in enhanced'

John Nowland

Barrie Tucker's packaging for Saddler's Creek muscat and sauternes
Left Steff Geissbuhler's poster promoting the centennial of the New York Public Library

'The answer to this question varies from place to place. In some countries, design is part of the social ethic but in other countries it is seldom understood. This means it is often treated as an optional extra and a frivolous waste of money. Design can be a major communication tool providing enough designers extol the passion and virtue that this medium can offer. Society, overall, would be the beneficiary'

Michael Peters

Wickens Tutt Southgate's packaging
for Billington's designed by
Ruth Waddingham
Opposite John Warwicker's stills
from a video designed with Tomato

'Firstly, get rid of the words 'graphic design'. Be more specific: visual communication: typographic communication: typological communication...'

John Warwicker

'I think this varies from country to country but the answer is generally no, there is not a good understanding. As long as our clients and the business community understand it, and as long as consumers respond to it by, for example, buying the packaging we design, I think that there is little need for society in general to have a better understanding of design.

There is however, a need for better education of the client community so that they can understand how to get the best from us. This is not so much that they need to understand how design works but more that they need to understand how to manage the process so that it does what we promise them it will do. In the UK this is being addressed through industry bodies such as the Design Council, the Design Business Association and the designers and Art Directors Association. However, the efforts of bodies like these need to be enhanced by the design community in general. As a passionate believer in the power of design I lay the blame for business lack of understanding firmly at the feet of the design industry. It has, historically, too often undermined itself by selling itself short, producing cheap, sub-standard work. Obviously this is not true of quality design companies but it is proof of how the actions of a few can create a harder job for the majority. It is consequently necessary to get the design community to promote itself with the stature it deserves before we can expect the client community to appreciate how powerful design can be'

Mark Wickens

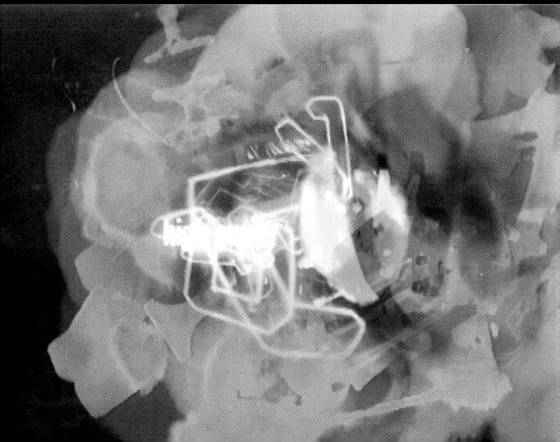

RIGHTSofHUMANKIND

Design & Illustration by Shin Matsunaga

'Do good work. People see what you show them; if you are a good communicator with wit and something to say, they'll get it. If you want to improve society's view of graphic designers there's only one way: produce better designs. It takes determination, intelligence and skill. You can't buy that and you certainly won't find it inside a computer'

Henry Steiner

'I think there is. However, it would be unwise to totally negate the huge potential of computers in the years to come. Core ideas come from within the human mind, and the computer is actually a rational new tool derived from one such idea. Computers have become extremely valuable in expanding our range of expression and accelerating the world process'

Shin Matsunaga

'I think that in Japan graphic design is understood by about ninety per cent of the population. School art textbooks contain a section on design (functional form). Graphic design is promoted here through children's poster contests, and in general through the staging of social and cultural poster exhibitions which bring people much enjoyment'

Shigeo Fukuda

'Graphics are everywhere. Life itself can be seen graphically as photography. If you read, there's always something to read. Magazines are seen in every culture on earth. So everyone knows what graphics are even if they don't call them graphics. 'Today most people can see the difference between what they think is a good ad and what they think is a bad one. Well-designed packaging certainly works better than poor packaging although designers may always argue about what's good and what isn't. Book jackets today are much better and more sensual than they were ten years ago. They wouldn't be if people didn't appreciate the value of graphic design. But in many important areas of life, like Health Care and Social Security, graphics and the language of forms and other communications still has a long way to go. There's plenty of work for ambitious graphic designers in design for print of all sorts, signs of all sorts, products of all sorts and multimedia. If road signs and tax forms and government materials become wonderful, helpful, friendly and even entertaining, 'society's' view of our work will improve'

Michael Wolff

Shigeo Fukuda's poster for Artis 89 entitled 'Les Droits de L'Homme'
Opposite Shin Matsunaga's poster for Artis 89 entitled 'Rights of Humankind'

These things make V23 tick. Pele, Robert LePage, Jaques Tati, Gerard Manley Hopkins, Cucumber sandwiches and fisticuffs, Sigmar Polke, Bird Island, Richard Misrach, Reeves and Mortimer, Sergie Paradjanov, Robert Doisneau, Sally Gunnell, Gaudi, Mark Rothko, Ivo Watts-Russell, David Lynch, Aubrey Beardsley, Tommy Cooper, Samuel Beckett, Joseph Beuys, Joy Division, Len Shackleton, Acupuncture, Faith, True Stories: Vernon, Florida, Antoni Tapies, The British Milers Club, Gulliver's Travels, Tokyo Salamander, Andrei Tarkovsky, Pere Ubu, Morecambe and Wise, Slipping Glimpser, Joan Fontecuberta, Martin Parr, Robe O'Connor, Arvo Part, Howard Devoto, Agfa Repromaster mk3, Secrets of the Beehive, Christian Boltankski, Ralph Eugene Meatyard, Max Wall, A Clockwork Orange, Guinness, Lee Friedlander, Against Nature, Nanking W6, Natural Wonders of the tropical marine world viewed with the aid of scuba equipment, Phillipe Decouflé, Tomato, Robert Rauchenberg, Russell Bagley's Box, CRDC Nantes, David Byrne, True Stories, Raygun, Pixies Live, Nick Drake, Ecstasy, Anselm Kiefer, Fischi and Weiss, Chain Reaction, Terry Dowling, Track 7, George Carl, Shinro Ohtake, Joel-Peter Witkin, Brian Eno, The Quay Brothers, Sankai Juku, Lust for Life, Emigre, put it in the bag ginger

Vaughan Oliver

'Cities, sound, a hybrid of
the organic and digital, it all
seems to add up to something,
does it? We've no idea how
it works and it's pointless to
try. The basis of our work is
individual experimentation
with form, structure and
language. We encourage
each other to blur not only
the responses to any given
situation but also the
methods and models of
working. The main objective
of our communal existence
is to enable and support each
others' journeys. The work is
the map of our individual and
collective experience'

Tomato

Q

How do the concepts for new design styles come about? Can it sometimes be accidental or through someone taking a risk?

'The question of risk is a complex one, particularly when it applies to aesthetics. Everybody in the design world celebrates the idea of risk but enjoys punishing people when they fail. Design risks are modest and usually their worst consequences are humiliation. This can be embarrassing but scarcely life-threatening. Clients are very often risk-adverse, understandably, because they have much to lose. New design styles usually come about through someone's small accomplishments in suggesting a new path. There is a kind of blood lust in some to be on the cutting edge in our society, and if a graphic form seems to be changing, the magazines and periodicals stumble over themselves to celebrate. This in turn creates a trend, and we are off to a new hemline. It is all driven by the essential economic determinism of consumer capitalism that employs the design ideas that originate among the talented for its own purposes'

Milton Glaser

'Design, by definition, is the giving of form to a thought, to a concept. One could therefore reasonably expect that all original forms engender original designs, or inversely, that original forms question cultural certitudes and classifications. I think that it is under collective historical and/or social pressure that the necessary fusing of form and substance operates and gives birth to style. But it's the midwife at each birth who takes the risk of the research. The fruit of chance and necessity, styles erupt like accidental acts upon their first public appearance but are quickly experienced as ordinary reality by the ensemble of contemporaries'

Pierre Bernard

'The concepts for design styles well up instantaneously in my brain and the source that initiates the instruction is unknown to me. I always try it whether it is accidental or taking a risk'
Makoto Saito

'Challenge to each new design'
Makoto Saito

'Design theory evolves while design styles are ephemeral and therefore not interesting to me. I despise obsolescence'
Massimo Vignelli

Makoto Saito's poster promoting Alpha Cubic Company Ltd, a fashion boutique

'By being alive'
John Warwicker

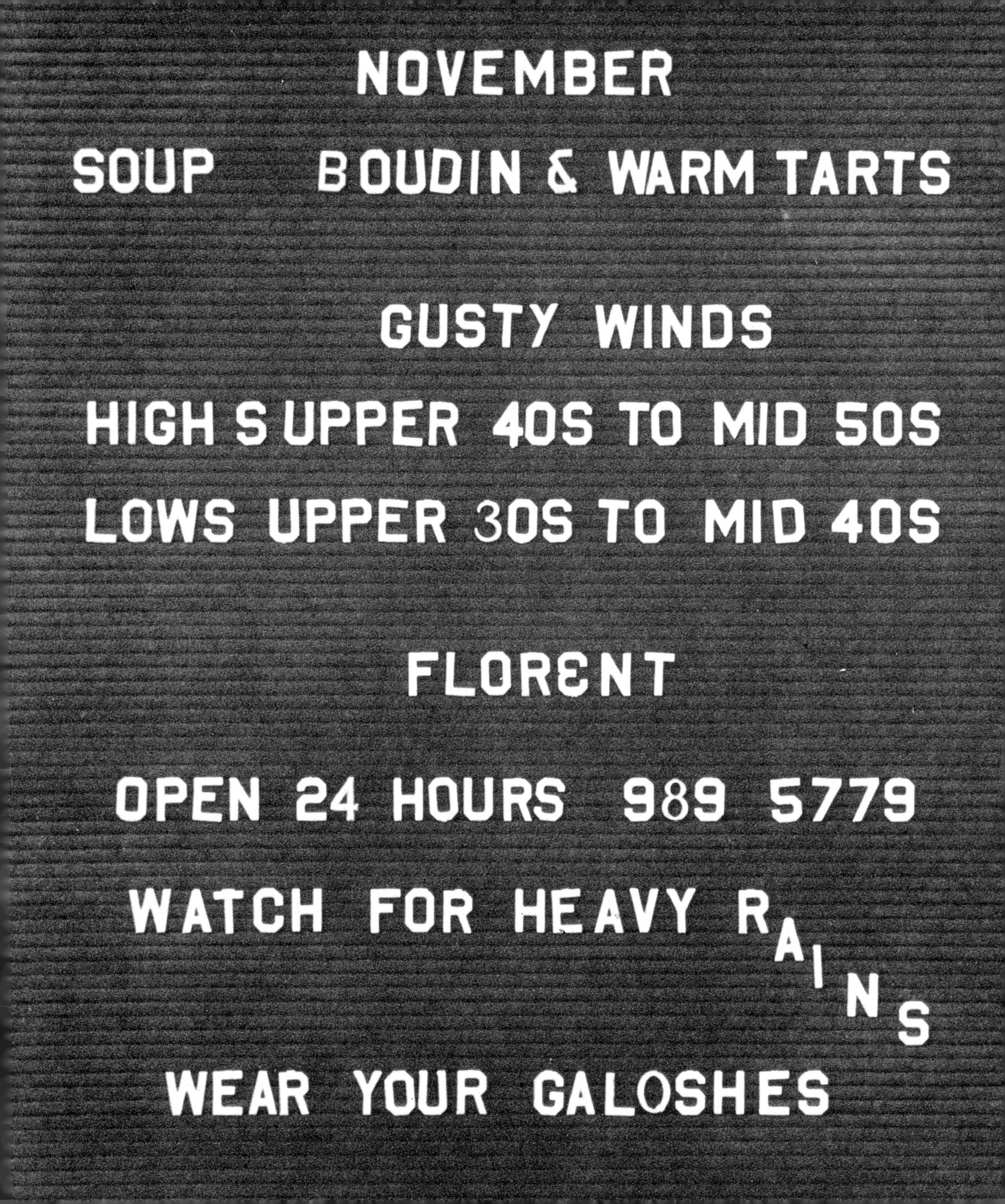

NOVEMBER

SOUP   BOUDIN & WARM TARTS

GUSTY WINDS

HIGHS UPPER 40S TO MID 50S

LOWS UPPER 30S TO MID 40S

FLORENT

OPEN 24 HOURS 989 5779

WATCH FOR HEAVY RAINS

WEAR YOUR GALOSHES

'New styles come about when somebody invents, hits a nerve and gets copied. It is always either accidental or subconscious, and always involves someone taking a risk. (Clients take much bigger risks than designers; they've got something at stake - they lose their jobs)'

Tibor Kalman

'By definition creativity comes from nowhere. You have to be an empty room, waiting for accident or inspiration. Reaction, which drives most design, comes from somewhere. Usually from you, anxious, ambitious to get it right, competitive, pressed for time and scheming room. Most design is derivative, and based on reason or precedent. In other words it's meant to be low-risk and not creative. For me creativity is essential in design. But it's unpredictable and risky. It produces ideas and concepts that aren't even recognisable as solutions so you can look foolish and naive to your clients unless they know and trust you. Few design companies are interested in creativity these days because it's far easier to repeat and sell their formulas for analysis and design. Creativity is more common among relatively innovative companies in industries like bio-technology and computing. I find much of the design business stuck in a rut. It has been for some time. It will have to become more creative soon in order to bring more profound value to its clients than it does today'

Michael Wolff

Alan Fletcher's cover design for 'Domus' promoting the Milan Furniture Fair
Opposite Tibor Kalman's cover for 'Colors'

Someone seeing things in a new way.

Alan Fletcher

Q

What is the solution for an 'ideas design block'?

'Most problems are boring. You cannot have an interesting solution to a boring problem. You must first turn the boring problem into an interesting one'

Bob Gill

'Steal'

Bob Gill

Steal someone else's.

Alan Fletcher

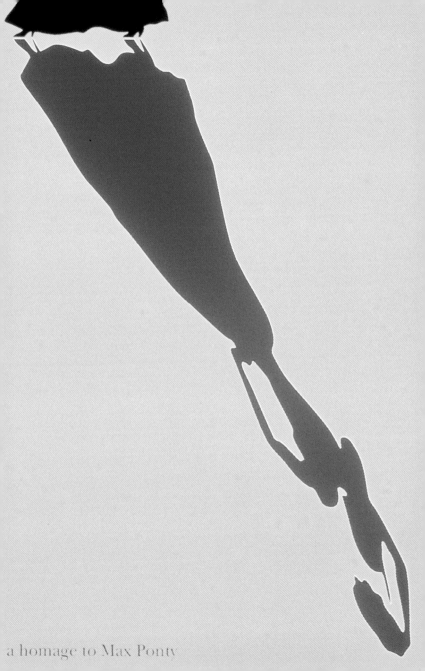

a homage to Max Ponty

CHOCOLATE
MINT
ALMONDS

CRUNCHY, WHOLE,
TOASTED CALIFORNIA
ALMONDS LAVISHLY
COATED WITH RICH
BITTERSWEET CHOCO-
LATE AND FINISHED
WITH MINTED WHITE
CHOCOLATE.

COCOLAT
BERKELEY, CALIFORNIA 94710

BITTERSWEET
CHOCOLATE
RAISIN BARK

SWEET, SUNRIPENED
RAISINS IN RICH, BIT-
TERSWEET CHOCOLATE
FOR CONNOISSEURS AND
SERIOUS NIBBLERS.
IRRESISTIBLE.

COCOLAT
BERKELEY, CALIFORNIA 94710

TRIPLE
CHOCOLATE
ALMONDS

CRUNCHY, WHOLE,
FRESH TOASTED CALI-
FORNIA ALMONDS LAV-
ISHLY COATED WITH
RICH, BITTERSWEET
AND MILK CHOCOLATES
AND DUSTED WITH THE
FINEST DUTCH COCOA.

COCOLAT
BERKELEY, CALIFORNIA 94710

'Visit a museum, tread on foreign land, escape to nature, ponder by a pool, or, when all else fails, wait until the last minute (that always does the trick!)'

Jennifer Morla

1 Think of something else. Nothing is worse than worrying about it
2 Approach the problem from a new perspective. Turn it on its head
3 Take yourself out of context. Away from the studio. Alternative criteria will have an impact on the subliminal creative thought.
Finally, when the blank sheet of paper confronts me I tell myself that we've been here before and can do it again'

Mary Lewis

Opposite Jennifer Morla's packaging for Cocolat, a range of gourmet confectionery
Below Mary Lewis's identity system for the Geffrye Museum

EDUCATION

LIBRARY

HERB GARDEN

MEN

GALLERIES

INFORMATION

COFFEE BAR

WOMEN

IMAGES OF ILLUSION
SHIGEO FUKUDA
1984

Shigeo Fukuda's poster for his
exhibition 'Images of Illusion' held
at the Isetan Museum
Opposite Milton Glaser's poster for
the Society of Newspaper Designers

'A distraction, an adventure, an
encounter, a walk, a swim, a
conversation with a child, and most
of all letting go of the idea with which
you're struggling. Change the subject.
Go outside and look at a flower. Try to
see it for the first time in a different way.
Marvel at it, smell it, surrender to it.
I usually find all blocks are caused by
old favoured ideas that get in the way
and intrude in the empty space that I
need in order to be creative'

Michael Wolff

'I am a professional graphic designer,
and hence do not have blocks. I am
constantly studying and striving to
overcome blocks; every day, morning,
noon and night. That is because I am
a professional'

Shigeo Fukuda

Talent

John Warwicker

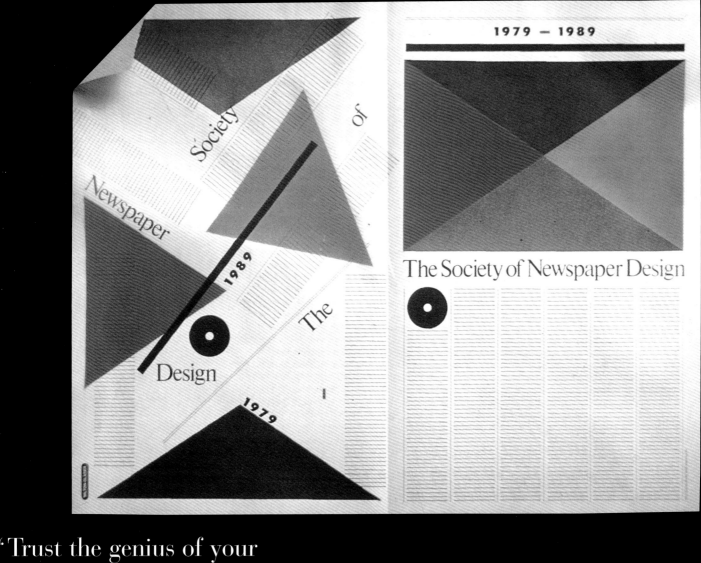

"Trust the genius of your
imagination and give it
the time it wants to
produce answers for you.
Have enough skill and
training to be able to

'It all depends on the complexity as well as the design requirements of each project. At times, the finished art will be best done by the designers in order to achieve the specific effect that he/she has in mind, especially nowadays when the majority of artwork is executed on the computer. In most cases and under normal circumstances, finished art should be done by the finished artists. However, one must bear in mind that there are two types of artists - one who does only straight-forward paste-up work and the other who is a lot more artistic and can actually help to improve the layout proportion for the designers'

Alan Chan

'I don't think there's any one way of doing things that's right. However you do it, use the best. And even if it isn't you, never forget that you are responsible for the finished job. You can never blame anyone else'

Michael Wolff

'I have worked with very good designers who can't draw, wouldn't know what 'finished art' is, and who balk at the sight of a magic marker (or even a pencil). But the excellent ones have, almost without exception, understood or practised the basics'

Mary Lewis

Should designers be doing their own finished art or should design be left for designers and finished art done by finished artists?

Mary Lewis's packaging for BHS
Opposite Alan Chan's packaging for Kosta Boda

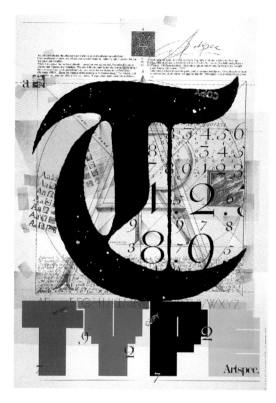

'What does it matter? The design process is a continuum: who does what is of little consequence, other than for the purpose of effective management, and it naturally depends on the size of the design office and the nature of the projects. All skills are important'

Garry Emery

'Personally, I have learnt so much from following my ideas from concept to board and liaising with the printer. New ideas are often borne at the colour spec or mark-up stage. That is, a specification such as printing the magenta values as metallic puce can totally affect the look of a job but it can only be arrived at through total involvement in the finished art stage'

Vaughan Oliver

Above Garry Emery's poster promoting a lecture series on type for Artspec
Steff Geissbuhler's poster entitled 'Peace' commemorating 40 years since the bombing of Hiroshima

'In our office we used to believe that our designers should design and our production people should produce mechanicals. However, the computer has changed all that, in that the final design is the final art and mechanical, often in the form of an electronic file. However, if the art is very complex, we have specialists who can do a faster and better job on a project and they will work with the designer in producing that. We still retain hands-on production personnel for old fashioned mechanicals, preparation of presentations and building of models'

Steff Geissbuhler

'There are no should or should nots in design. I personally do not have the interest or the computer expertise necessary to do finished mechanical art. Design is the conceptual process not the mechanical specifics. Leave the mechanical process to the pros. But do expect and demand attention to all details from the beginning to end of each project'

Jennifer Morla

'Today, a lot of finished art is computer-generated but quality design still relies on the special skills of both designers and craftsmen. If the designer creates something that can only be executed by him/herself, or if the design involves the work of an illustrator, it is essential that they be involved in the production of the finished art and that it is not merely computer generated'

Michael Peters

'I don't believe that designers should produce their own finished art for the simple reason that it is not the best use of their time. Designers should spend their time problem solving, being creative, having ideas and crafting great work. All the design decisions on a job should have been made by the time a piece of work gets to artwork stage, so it is better to allow the designer to be creative with the next task, rather than be mechanical in finishing off this task. Rather than do artwork themselves 'to make sure it is right' designers need art direction skills to enable others to realise their work. They also need sufficient digital artwork understanding to be able to hand over their work to a digital artist on a form with which the latter can quickly and easily work'

Mark Wickens

' Both, whatever is most appropriate'

Massimo Vignelli

Wickens Tutt Southgate's packaging for BHS tinted glassware, designed by Clem Halpin
Opposite Jennifer Morla's design for 'Espresso' for Sara Slavin, Karl Petze and Chronicle Books

Ham and Eggs. 'Design is what happens between conceiving an idea and fashioning the means to carry it out. Whether it's the big stuff, like painting a picture, writing a novel, conducting a military battle or creating a commercial enterprise; or small stuff, like re-organising a room. In short, design is an intelligent equation between purpose and construction. A few people also earn their living by giving form to the amenities of life in manufacture, communication and place. They call themselves designers. They are the blue collar workers of the art world.

Whereas painters are concerned with solving their own problems, designers occupy themselves solving other people's problems. Actually that's an over-simplification. Their aim goes beyond finding a solution; it's the elegance of the solution that counts. That's a personal challenge rather than utilitarian discipline. A commitment rather than an involvement. A difference exampled by a plate of ham and eggs. Here the pig is committed whereas the chicken is merely involved. 'Designers derive their rewards from 'inner standards of excellence', from the intrinsic satisfaction of their tasks. They are committed to the task, not the job; to their standards, not to their boss. So whereas most people divide their lives between time spent earning money and more time spending it, designers generally lead seamless existences. As designer Richard Sapper neatly put it, 'I never work - all the time"

Alan Fletcher

'I suppose the only true Australian design comes from the first Australians - the Aborigines. Their paintings and marks cover this great land from one side to the other. For thousands of years they have been making marks without any outside interference. The newcomers arrived here from many different parts of the world and are still coming, bringing with them the usual differences such as language. The outside influences are many and come thick and fast; it's global marketing homogenising cultural differences. Down the track I am sure that evolution will help develop a mood or a look in what we call Australian design. If design were a sport we would be seen in a different light on the world stage. To think Paul Klee said 'One eye looks, the other feels''

David Lancashire

'Yes. And No. For instance I think 'Strictly Ballroom' and 'Muriel's Wedding' are both wonderful, and Australian, movies. But they're great international movies by any standards. They happen to be about Australian circumstances and they happen to have an Australian flavour. By whatever criteria you use, good design is good, and bad design is bad anywhere'

Michael Wolff

Q

Is there such
a thing as
'Australian design'?

David Lancashire's signage for
Marrawuddi Gallery
Opposite David Lancashire's signage
for the Bowali Visitor Centre

'Australian design? I don't believe there is such a thing as Australian design 'style', not at this stage anyway. I believe that the very best of Australian design is indeed 'international' design. The very best of Australian design can hold its own anywhere in the world; that has been proven and will continue to do so. I am not sure exactly how 'Australian design' is seen overseas. It is up to an overseas designer to comment. As Australia's population is so small there isn't the quantity of quality designers to force a huge impact on the world of design. I believe that young Australian designers should think for themselves. They should create concepts based on their own experiences, surroundings and abilities, and not rely on books from overseas to simply copy solutions created by a designer from another part of the world. The very best of Australian design is created by thinking, creative Australian designers desirous of pushing their abilities progressively forward.

I do not think there has to be a conscious effort amongst Australian designers as a 'group' to concoct a design style where all Australian design finally looks the same. It has been done elsewhere in the world and has been publicised considerably but overall I don't think that it is a healthy thing. Let us strive to make the design produced in Australia noticeable to the rest of the world through quality innovative concepts and the quality of the final products. Well that's the personal aim of Barrie Tucker!'

Barrie Tucker

David Lancashire's packaging for Eureka Farm Produce
Right Barrie Tucker's packaging for Nautilus cabernet sauvignon merlot (Negociants New Zealand)

'Yes, and how! Australian designers are lively. There is no reason for having an Australian design. Design is one, the world over, otherwise it is provincial and not good'

Massimo Vignelli

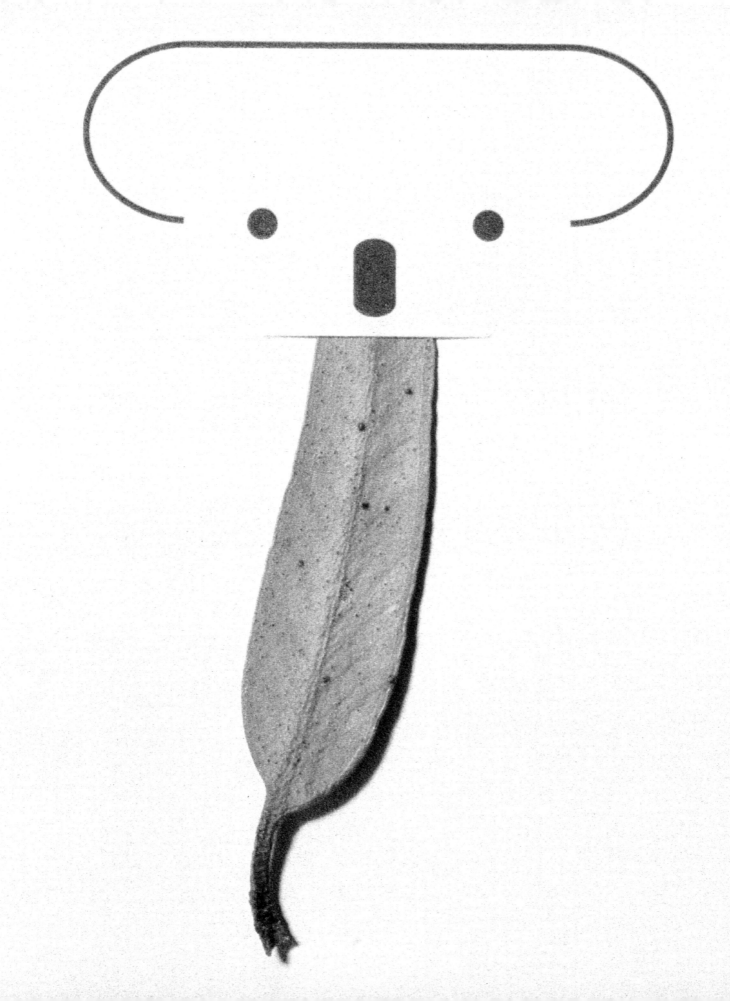

'Not noticeably because there has been no consistent and related development in our education system. Design as a recognised discipline in Australia has developed over the last 40-odd years. There has been considerable change and exchange so a distinctly Australian approach has not yet been established. I believe there is a definite Australian attitude; a freshness, a willingness to try, to explore, to invent because we are not 'hampered' by an 'approach'. Ironically, there are noticeable differences between the states of Australia. I'm not sure if this is in response to the character of communities, including their education, business opportunities, given climate or attitudes, but the differences are there'

John Nowland

'Design is an integral part of industry. Having items such as places, goods or products that are merely recognised as tourist icons does not mean they incorporate design. Creations that emerge from industry form part of a culture, which in turn determines design. I have yet to meet with Australian design'

Shigeo Fukuda

'Like any good design, there isn't a national 'look' to it because Australian designers are creating solutions to business problems, rather than creating 'looks' for the sake of them. In some countries there have been design movements which have created a 'look', for example in Holland, but I have not observed this happening in Australia'

Mark Wickens

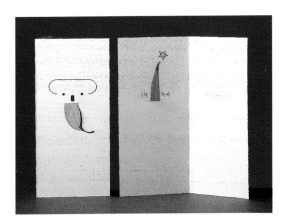 

John Nowland's self-promotional
Christmas card design

Q

What would you say is the biggest threat facing the design industry today?

'The biggest threats:
1. Resistance to change
2. Lack of knowledge of the world, of cultural, ethical, philosophical and intellectual concerns and of developments beyond the design profession
3. Technology that makes graphic communication available instantaneously and cheaply to everyone
4. Clients who are increasingly motivated to 'bottom-line-only' thinking
5. Middle management, unaware of the hidden opportunities, can sanction average, safe and familiar solutions
6. Therefore, 'pushing the envelope' (that great designers naturally try to achieve) is often considered a negative
7. An increasing tendency to view designers as interchangeable. They are not
8. Complacency ranks high on the danger list
9. Fear of risk'

Deborah Sussman

'Dumb designers. I have no sympathy for the consuming fascination with rending illegible the inconsequential. Nor can I derive gratification from a trite image of a fedora: people who have nothing to say should shut up. Technology is not responsible for the crisis facing our infant profession, any more than munitions are responsible for the former Yugoslavia; education is.
If physicians were schooled and trained like most graphic designers, there'd be no population explosion problem today'

Henry Steiner

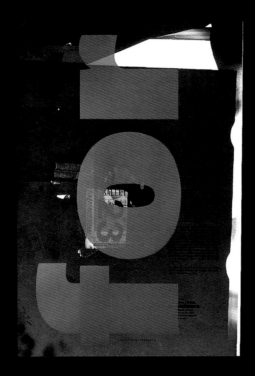

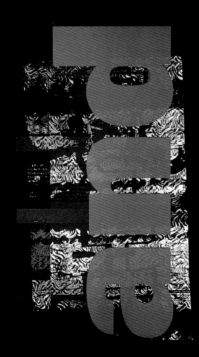
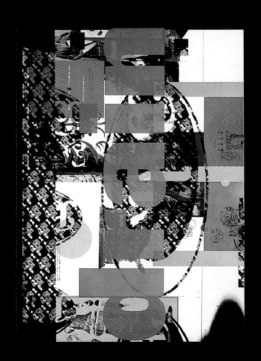

'Two things
1 Re-appropriation (plagiarism).
   Give me new soil, fresh bulbs
2 Another threat to the future of our
   industry comes from a tendency in
   design education to suppress the
   individual in favour of guiding students
   towards 'fitting in' with current trends so
   that finding a job upon graduation is a
   little easier. I mean that in college shows
   I'd like to see a lot more experimentation
   and individuality, rather than an ability
   to re-iterate current stylistic trends'

Vaughan Oliver

'Complacency and being too easily
satisfied by the approval of peers are
threats. The glittering awards syndrome.
Even more dangerous are the habits of
design companies; especially the habit of
thinking that they're right. The biggest
threat is being stuck in ways of thinking
and working because it seems more
comfortable than the challenge and
dislocation of constantly creating new
points of view. Change is always
happening around you but, like the
story of the frog in gradually boiling
water, you don't always notice it. A frog
dropped in scorching water will jump
out immediately. Left in cold water
and gradually brought to a boil it
comfortably falls asleep and gets cooked.
That's why designers don't take the
environmental threat seriously. It's not
warming up fast enough yet. It seems
like someone else's fire alarm, possibly
false and not the deadly blazing fire in
your house that it actually is. Any firm
that has a set way of doing things and
doesn't notice the changes warming up
around it better watch out!'

Michael Wolff

'The accessibility of design. What we do
is precious and private. Technology has
invaded that privacy and the signs of
abuse are there. Overly sophisticated
students. Armed with computer skills
they sell their wares mechanically and
strategically. Career paths are often
higher on their agenda than honing their
talent. Our creative experimental youth
is vital. Those in design education need
to get closer to the industry's real needs.
The proliferation of design 'stuff'.
Still cruising after the design boom of
the 80's, too many designers produce
average work by recognising and
exploiting the client comfort factor.
We need an energy force from within
the design and client community to
constantly change the goal posts and
ensure our legacy is one we are proud of'

Mary Lewis

'My first thought was of 'change' as
the biggest threat but it is the greatest
challenge. To feel threatened is to behave
defensively. My personal feeling of a
'threat' facing the design industry is that
our design graduates are not being given
an education appropriate to change; that
their work is becoming superficial rather
than thoughtful; manipulation rather
than curiosity; and technology rather
than intelligence'

John Nowland

Opposite Layouts from the Limited
Edition Catalogue for V23
John Nowland's brochure for the State
Opera of South Australia

'Malaria, global warming'

John Warwicker

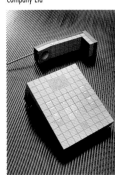

'Recession'

Takenobu Igarashi

'I believe that the greatest threat facing the design industry today is design itself especially when it serves, without restraint, the dominant world order of marketing. During the last century, in our so-called developed society, mass production has become organised and structured around a single objective - that of generating profit whenever it is possible. Different banners of progress have often hidden a deep and systematic disrespect for the general well-being of humankind. Numerous national and specific cultures have been despoiled when they've not been just simply eradicated. 'Like a steamroller on a one-way street, a global economy is suddenly put into place, preceeded and accompanied by the communications media, which is developing on the same scale. It is within this context of unequal exchange in the world market that we must consider the future of design and the special role of each of us as designers. Design is a sensitive and singular production of meaning in a society; each act of design is above all a cultural act. The social existence of design is far older than the concept itself. For these two reasons, every culture in the world is worthy of interest. Borne by its own history, each develops its specific energy. Each should have the right to participate in the general concert. From this perspective, in the same way that protection of the environment is being organised, it is becoming urgent to clearly preserve the access and contribution of every culture to universal culture. Because the best way to communicate is to broaden one's own culture, I think that design has a decent future only if it develops responsibly within a local framework. Under these conditions, if generalised democracy is to progress, the North/South and East/West dialogues, with everybody present, could be organised and perhaps attain what Walter Gropius stated not so long ago: 'Unity within diversity"

Pierre Bernard

'Make it look like theirs!'

Michael Wolff

'It's extraordinary that in business, where differentiation gets harder to sustain and essential to achieve, so many companies still prefer the comfort of hiding in conformity and looking much like their competitors. Having the job of drawing out authentic self-expression with a company, so that it looks like itself, and no-one else, in everything it does, is one of the most exhilarating privileges for any Designer'
Michael Wolff

'No two jobs are similar. Even when they appear to be alike they have different problems. The most common request is to achieve the best possible solution at the lowest possible price. Some clients, however, realise the real value of design because they understand the role that design can play in solving commercial problems. Remember, the client needs to help. Truly committed clients see design as a vital ingredient in the marketing mix; more importantly they see it as a tool to increase their company's profitability'
Michael Peters

'The most frequent concern or request is 'Make it readable!'
Steff Geissbuhler

Michael Peter's logotype for Mercury One 2 One, a telecommunications company
Left Steff Geissbuhler's corporate identity for National Public Radio

'There are various kinds of briefings and requests by clients

A

Type A is the one who thinks advertising or graphic design will solve their problems. In their briefing they have a lot of undefined requests and wishes. They have much deeper problems in their company that cannot be solved with only a graphic design solution. We advise them to analyse internal problems such as product quality, price and distribution politics, and to devise an innovative strategy

Jean Robert's designs for Swatch/ SMH developed with Kati Durrer

B

Type B is the one who likes to get the same solution we designed successfully for another client! We advise them to reconsider their wishes and tell them that together we have to work out a briefing for an adequate design solution

C

Type C is the ideal one who comes to us with an open mind and a very good product or service. Their briefing provides good information and facts, which basically lead very easily to a good design solution. The most common good briefing is the one we develop with the client'

Jean Robert

'Clients need to be heard. They want, and deserve, to be listened to very carefully. Good clients can be flexible when they feel their needs are being attended to, more so than when designs produce spectacular work that does not meet their stated requirements. All clients respond to meeting budgets and deadlines; good clients also respect good design; great clients enable great work. They are rare, but they are there'

Deborah Sussman

'I would not say there is any particular request from clients at briefing stage especially in so-called 'design ideas or solutions'. Having worked as a designer in the wine industry for some time now, there was a period, maybe 15 years ago, when Australian wine did not have the international reputation it enjoys now. Then Australian wine companies were 'self-conscious' and worried about their rating against the French; every client who briefed in a wine label project stated up front 'make it look French'. Australian wine packaging designers have changed that! The French are now inviting us to show them how to put some excitement into their packaging'

Barrie Tucker

'In the area in which we specialise, branding, the most common request is for packaging which is both 'traditional' and 'modern'. What the client means is 'timeless''

Mark Wickens

Barrie Tucker's packaging for Bluegrass cabernet sauvignon for Saddlers Creek Winery, designed with Jody Tucker
Left Wickens Tutt Southgate's packaging for Gales Honey, designed by Allison Miguel
Opposite Deborah Sussman's logotype for Culver City Redevelopment Agency

'Follow your natural inclinations. Predicting the future is for politicians'

Bob Gill

'I've never been able to predict the future. Nevertheless, a guess. People tend to fulfil their inner needs and naturally gravitate toward certain modes. Two examples: some are intensely specific, linear and focused on avenues that are clear, describable and organised; others operate on several tracks simultaneously, even divergent ones, going back and forth and crossing over, often in service of 'big picture' concepts. There's room and need for both the specialist and the generalist (and those afflicted by both characteristics) in the future, just as there is now, and as there was in the past'
Deborah Sussman

'Hopefully both. They feed each other. You can't shut out diversity and there will always be more focus achieved in specialising. If you can be both a parent and a marathon runner, you can be a thinker with a broad view and a program-writing maniac'
Michael Wolff

'Working in a relatively small community (Adelaide) I have had to diversify by choice, need and opportunity. To survive, learn and develop, one must take opportunities as they present themselves'
John Nowland

John Nowland's packaging for
Sharefarmers Blend for
Petaluma Limited
Below Deborah Sussman's interiors
for the North Arcade for Gund
Investment Corporation

'Specialising
can only happen
after a very
good general
education.
A diversified
designer, most
of the time, is a
better designer'

Massimo Vignelli

Pierre Bernard's cover for 'Graphic
Design World Views' by Jorge Frascara
for ICOGRADA

'The only specialist skill that I see as necessary for the designer is knowing how to acquire the capacity for developing diverse skills'

Pierre Bernard

'One of the things that sets an artist, a graphic artist, apart is conviction; creating art or designing as if it mattered, as if the world mattered. Graphic design is generally held to be a minor art. Rather than transforming reality, a feat claimed by painters and sculptors, graphic design is seen as auxiliary to sales. Thirty years ago the public heard that the 'medium is the message'. Cool or hot. And the finest graphic designers have inscribed their messages in a variety of media. Saul Bass and Milton Glaser applied their artistry to film and aeroplanes as well as posters and annual reports. Innovative companies like Knoll understood that every product is a graphic, and collaborated with designers Vignelli and Sottsass to produce chairs that have become as 'classic' as Ionic columns. Knoll recognised that design was the tool needed to refine their products down to precise detail; designers developed and supported the company's stringent criteria of quality. Design was not a decoration in the service of sales, a way of dressing up the product in order to make it presentable. The uncompromising intelligence of Knoll's designers contributed in the most fundamental way to the success of the company, while the expression of the individual designer in uniquely beautiful products delighted the public. A decade ago, Paul Rand wrote 'It is no secret that the real world in which the designer functions is... the world of buying and selling... but without good design the marketplace would only be a showcase of visual vulgarity'. I agree. Especially

with the 'but' and I would only add that the graphic designer can be a positive force in transforming the marketplace and shaping a richer collective life. On the whole, I believe that the tie with business has been good for the profession. The demands of industry can inspire designers to come up with extraordinary solutions, ones that convince and delight. The pressure of designing within the confines of commercial necessity can produce the most highly-focused and exciting work. Designers serve clients just as renaissance artists bowed to the Pope or noblemen who commissioned a chapel fresco or tapestry. But like those artists, we cannot limit ourselves to the specific ends of solving the immediate problem. We must not fall prey to the cynical spirit of a decade that would have us believe that our work is just another disposable part of a trash culture. Good design requires the unfashionable qualities of feeling and commitment if it is to outlast the current trend of splicing styles and surfaces. Both designers and clients should know that good design can be more than just a visual fix or a sales pitch just as cathedrals, statuary and portraiture delivered more than their specific messages of wealth and power. It is perhaps only in the last century that art has been kicked upstairs into an ivory tower (where there's a very exclusive high-stakes game going on between collectors, curators and artists) cloistered in museums and collections, adored by critics and connoisseurs and CEOs like a golden calf. The posture of the artist as creative genius and the

Michael Vanderbyl's identity for the
Mead 60 Paper Competition

consuming interest in deals and image has both elevated and reduced fine art to a glamorous commodity. The fine arts are physically inaccessible to most of the public and aesthetically inaccessible as well. The public can no longer 'see' a painting because it lacks a critical education and the interpretive key of theory. Paintings are esoteric puzzles for an elite clique. If the style of post-modern art is a garage sale of perspectives, materials, genres and so on, the prices are certainly not. And if post-modern art has moved away from the 'silence' of modern minimalism, it still fails to speak to the public. It is neither seen nor heard in the real life of the community that goes on in the workplace, the shops and cafes. That's where you find graphic art, hanging out on street corners, in the corporate offices, public and private institutions, the retail environment, and in people's homes, informing, transforming, enlightening, and clarifying everyday life. Let's acknowledge the importance of the visual history and visual world created by graphic design in the artefacts and images with which we continually interact in our daily life. Why, after all, do we study the baskets, clay jars, religious objects and public architecture of a people? The artist leaves the imprint of his or her individual sensitivity in proportion, space and materials and his personal passions, strengths and flaws, but we also find there traces of the myths, traditions and social history of a culture, their sense of relatedness to each other and to nature. Just as our comic strips, neon signs, toasters, shoe boxes,

lipsticks, magazines and posters tell us about our science, our fantasies, our mating rituals, and so forth. The value of graphic design is tied not only to form and function but also to the feeling one has for life; our work as designers is not limited to specific functional or educational ends. We can contribute directly to the pleasure, ease and colour of life, the way life feels. Designers not only open the channels of desire with seductive images, or streamline tasks with models of efficiency. Designers can no longer think of themselves as simply engineers of information, tools of the corporate world or marketing strategies. We must find sources of self-expression and meaning as well as solving problems. The trend has been to look outside and into the past for inspiration, borrowing from other times and tribes, but we can also turn inside by exploring personal feeling and memory, our own passions, our own ironic sense of humanity and of tragedy, our own hungers, anxieties and pleasures. In this way, our design will be not only accessible and appropriate but also truly new, interesting and meaningful. Design can inspire us as individuals, move us as members of a world community, help us to achieve understanding, enhance our work, make us laugh, give us pleasure, startle, surprise and prevent us from being swamped in a 'showcase of… vulgarity'. We must also contribute something of a long-lasting worth alongside the daily life in the fast track. Not content to passively render mere fragments of style, our personal commitment to design can serve to inspire us all to think that it does matter'

Michael Vanderbyl

What is your definition of design? If you have more than one, which one applies to yourself the most?

'As an artist, design is the medium that I have chosen to express my art. Hopefully, at its best, design is art. At its worst, it merely solves the problem. Design is everything you see, experience and touch'

Michael Vanderbyl

'To define good design is to combine many elements of a problem. Putting them together, and in the right order, creates a solution to the problem we have been asked to solve'

Jean Robert

'Design is style with content and content with style'

Jennifer Morla

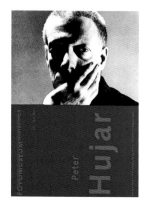

Jean Robert's posters promoting exhibitions at the Fotomuseum
Right Tibor Kalman's album cover design for Defunkt
Opposite Tibor Kalman's album cover design for David Byrne

'Graphic design is the typographic organisation of information; space, scale and sequence are the most important elements for me. Which is no small undertaking!'

Massimo Vignelli

'Design is two things: invention; and styling. We need a lot more of the former and a lot less of the latter'

Tibor Kalman

DAVID BYRNE

3 BIG SONGS

45 RPM

BIG BUSINESS

MY BIG HANDS

BIG BLUE PLYMOUTH

'To me design has three distinct
and interrelated meanings
Design as an underlying context. A big
picture, a vision, a grand design. Like
Paris. Or like Apple. For instance, the
idea behind Apple was to put the power
of the personal computer in the hands of
every individual on the planet. Maybe
impossible to achieve. But it's why they
created the Apple attitude and why
they had to pioneer the extraordinary
Macintosh interface

Design as the quality of an object.
For instance L'Arc de Triomphe.
Or the design of the original, friendly
little Apple Macintosh, the 'Beetle'
of computers. Or the design of the
definitive Macintosh launch commercial.
Fifty Macintoshes sitting in a classroom
learning about human behaviour. It was
the antithesis of the IBM idea where
humans sit in the classroom learning
with difficulty about the esoteric and
technical world of computers

Design is a process. It's the means of
ensuring that vision or the grand design
is expressed in all the details that
represent it. For instance the process that
ensures the coherence of the Apple way
of doing things and the characteristic
Apple look in everything they produce.
From ads to manuals, from the mouse to
the smiling icon on the screen, the design
of the little bitten apple is the tip of an
iceberg of absolute consistency'

Michael Wolff

'My definition of design
1 Relevant creativity, skillfully applied
2 The shape of things to come
3 A language, a communicator, a need
4 Problem solving at its most simplistic
5 Changing the world, at its most profound'

Mary Lewis

'Unlike art, there are many restrictions on design. By working only to resolve problems arising from these restrictions your work is merely a business transaction. I believe it is most important to incorporate something of yourself in each work, something that only you can contribute'

Shigeo Fukuda

Mary Lewis's packaging for Journey, a male fragrance

'In a workshop run by Milton Glaser, we reached a working definition of design as 'meaningful intervention in process'. This is pretty broad but sits quite nicely with my view that our function is to give form to ideas and meaning to form. It's nice if the design raises the spirit. I tend to want to keep things as simple as possible'

Brian Sadgrove

Brian Sadgrove's symbol for Yarra Valley Water for Melbourne Water
Opposite Shin Matsunaga's poster for the Japan Graphic Designers Association entitled 'Peace'

'Even when of superior colour or form, in the end, what makes a design work is its substance. Good designs make visible the achievements and actions of the products they represent. Often in the creative process, an aspect (such as colour or form) dominates but once completed, balance is the key to making a design shine. Unless unusually limited or specific, designs are based on the human lifestyle, and it is natural for them to have personality. And only with such personality does a design ultimately become successful. A design is, in a sense, similar to a human face; it mirrors personality and is full of expression. These forms of expression are infinite. One appeals strongly but the content is poor, whilst another has superior originality but is very quiet and silent. I believe that content will ultimately prevail. Achieving excellence in design is the result of pursuing every possibility and process to bring impressions to reality. It is important not to miss any chance or effort to find that. I enjoy discovering the existence of something totally fresh and new, in spite of my initial impression that it may be ordinary, not mysterious or unusual. Encountering such a moment yields the realisation of my designs'

Shin Matsunaga

'The business of graphic design is much more than organising image, colour, text, scale and proportion into a harmonious whole. We deal with problems. To develop visual solutions that are appropriate and distinguishing, they need to be communicable, understood and effective. Such solutions are the result of listening, curiosity, experience and hard work'

John Nowland

PEACE

LOVE, PEACE, AND HAPPINESS.

Joining "HIROSHIMA APPEALS 1986" / Design & Illustration by Shin Matsunaga

Printed in Japan by Toppan Printing Co., Ltd.

Acknowledgements
This volume has been made possible through the contribution of questions from many students from many colleges, from many countries. The coordination of the material both in terms of questions and responses has been assembled by Heather Wellard. The responses to the questions have come with the generous assistance of Pierre Bernard, Alan Chan, Garry Emery, Alan Fletcher, Shigeo Fukuda, Steff Geissbuhler, Bob Gill, Milton Glaser, Roz Goldfarb, Takenobu Igarashi, Tibor Kalman, David Lancashire, Mary Lewis, Shin Matsunaga, Jennifer Morla, John Nowland, Vaughan Oliver, Michael Peters, Jean Robert, Brian Sadgrove, Makoto Saito, Henry Steiner, Deborah Sussman, Erik Spiekermann, Barrie Tucker, Michael Vanderbyl, Massimo Vignelli, John Warwicker, Mark Wickens and Michael Wolff. Thank you for your hindsight. My thanks also go to Sue Stansfield and Friedo Ligthart for assembling the artwork and to Bridgette Newbury for editing. Also my thanks to the publishers, Craftsman House and in particular Nevill Drury for their dedication to provide quality publications for the design profession